What to Do When Your Students Talk Dirty

Timothy Jay, PhD

Resource Publications, Inc.
San Jose, California

Editorial director: Nick Wagner
Editor: Kenneth Guentert
Prepress manager: Elizabeth J. Asborno
Copyeditor: Leila T. Bulling

Reprint Department
Resource Publications, Inc.
160 E. Virginia Street #290
San Jose, CA 95112-5876
(408) 286-8505

Library of Congress Cataloging in Publication Data
Jay, Timothy.
    What to do when your students talk dirty / Timothy Jay.
      p.   cm.
    ISBN 0-89390-363-9 (pbk.)
    1. Classroom management—United States. 2. School children—United States—Discipline. 3. Swearing—United States. 4. English language—United States—Obscene words. 5. English language—United States—Slang. 6. Behavior modification—United States. I. Title.
LB3013.J39   1996
371.1'024—dc20   96-11898

Printed in the United States of America

00 99 98 97 96 | 5 4 3 2 1

CONTENTS

PART TWO: IDENTIFYING YOUR VALUES

PART THREE: SETTING STANDARDS

PART FIVE: IMPLEMENTING STANDARDS TO ELIMINATE CURSING

PART SIX: COPING WITH SPECIFIC PROBLEMS

PREFACE

Dirty words have been used in English for more than seven hundred years, and there is no reason to believe that they will disappear from usage. I wrote this book not to eliminate the use of dirty words but to provide classroom teachers with methods and strategies to reduce the use of cursing at school. Some forms of cursing are unacceptable and must not be used at all; one example is sexual harassment. Unacceptable language can be controlled with behavior management strategies. Other types of cursing, such as profanity, are inappropriate for use in the classroom, and students need to learn acceptable language to express their emotions. Teachers should instruct students about the etiquette of bad language (that is, why cursing is inappropriate) rather than attempt to eradicate cursing altogether, an impossible task.

The teacher's role is twofold:

1. a manager of behavior, using behavior management techniques to control language in the classroom

2. an instructor, teaching students how to use acceptable language in different contexts in society

The changes in students' attitudes and behavior over the last two decades have brought some unsettling problems into modern schools. Physical violence, drug use, illegal activities, sexual promiscuity, gang confrontations, and other incivilities now create a new level of stress for classroom teachers. Many teachers have not been prepared for and are not being trained to cope with difficult student behavior.

This book confronts a ubiquitous trend in modern times: the use of offensive language in public. You can control dirty word usage if you have adequate background information about the scope of the problem and a set of effective strategies to apply in particular circumstances. Internalizing the material in this book will increase your self-efficacy as a classroom teacher and reduce the amount of stress in your classes. As a result, you will gain a sense of control and achievement. Your students will lead more disciplined lives and, as a result, will be better able to cope with a wide variety of language and communication situations when they leave school.

Acknowledgments

I would like to thank Kenneth Guentert for his faith in this project and support throughout the production of the book. Thanks to the many teachers and students who provided information and guidance about instruction and management, especially Barbara Tatten, Jennifer Miller, and Jennifer Rotolo, who provided comments about the book during preliminary stages. I am deeply indebted to those teachers who took the time to review the entire book and give insightful comments: Starr Baker, Mary Ann Caproni, and Carol Cain.

I thank the principals and administrators who help set up Offensive Language workshops and assisted in collecting data regarding teachers' perceptions of language problems: Colleen Rossi, Joe Doyle, Linda Porter, and Joe Rogge. Thanks to Ed Filiault, who helped set up workshops for college credit through North Adams State College.

PART ONE

Identifying the Problem

CHAPTER 1

Dirty Words Have Many Colors

Every modern American on an average day is exposed to some type of cursing language. We hear dirty words on the street, at work, at school, on the radio, on the television, and in the home. Dirty words are just about everywhere we go. Every parent and teacher faces problems with children when they use dirty words. You cannot raise a modern child who never hears dirty language, and since Americans have been unable to eradicate offensive language, we must be prepared to deal with it. This book is designed to help you deal with bad language at school. I take the point of view that *every* teacher is a language teacher; I oppose the idea that correcting language is to be left to English and composition teachers alone. All must help to establish good speech habits.

The goal of the first part of the book is to introduce the variety of problems presented by middle school students' use of dirty words (also called "cursing"). I argue that students should learn to conform to conventional language norms; they should learn what might be called dirty word "etiquette." Word etiquette is the idea that cursing language represents a learned behavior which has appropriate, inappropriate, and unacceptable uses depending on context. Students need to learn the distinctions regarding acceptability and then speak accordingly. All teachers are responsible for helping students speak effectively and appropriately. We cannot just tell our students not to use certain words; we must be able to explain the consequences of inappropriate language usage to them.

Parents and teachers have a vested and shared interest in making sure children know the proper place of conventional language as well as the proper place of cursing language in contemporary society.

In the first part of the book I include examples and definitions of different kinds of dirty word problems (obscenity, profanity, vulgarity, harassment, etc.) that students and teachers experience. Cursing, as used generally, refers not to one type of word usage but several; each will be dealt with separately.

Word Etiquette

We all have a pretty good idea of what etiquette means. Etiquette is the acceptance of a set of rules, behaviors, conventions, and standards that guides our behavior and interactions with others. People adopt rules of etiquette that govern their appearance, social conduct, and speech. These conventions control the nature and scope of behavior in formal ceremonies and casual rituals. Etiquette is a conventional set of rules for conduct within situations and settings in society. Rules of etiquette include speaking and writing to others.

Etiquette exists to give people predictability and stability when they speak and interact with others. The ability to predict and anticipate what others are going to do or say gives us a sense of control. Without these rules life would be more stressful. For example, the chaos that might occur at the dinner table is replaced by a fairly rigid set of table manners. Obeying conventional table manners results in an orderly—that is, predictable—dinner ritual, in which both language and behavior are limited by etiquette.

The rules of etiquette not only define predictability but also define some behavior as appropriate and other behavior as inappropriate, rude, vulgar, embarrassing, or uncultured. Cursing falls into the category of behavior that is socially sanctioned and contextually restricted. Thus, our students and children need to learn the "rules of etiquette" of cursing—that is, when it is inappropriate and cannot be used (in my classroom!).

In all forms of communication, acknowledged and accepted conventions or standards must be followed if one is to be fully understood. Some of these rules are grammatical, like proper verb tenses, and some are social, like rules for addressing state officials (protocol). Our language customs have many layers of formality, from the very casual to the very formal. Choosing words is like choosing clothing; both come in different styles and levels of formality. Some manners of speaking, like some styles of clothing, are appropriate for one occasion, while alternative styles may be either too casual or too formal. Appropriateness in dress or speaking is a matter of style or formality.

Dirty words, especially the strong ones, are generally regarded as unacceptable in communication at school and in many public contexts. The term "unacceptable" means that the words are censored in a given context no matter how formal or relaxed. Unacceptable words should not be used at all. Less offensive words may be inappropriate for one context but not others. We may or may not hear some of these less offensive words in restricted settings.

How do we know dirty words are inappropriate or unacceptable? We are implicitly and explicitly told what is acceptable by those people who make communication rules. The language standard bearers are teachers, parents, government officials, mass media programming executives, religious figures, and community leaders. These authority figures decide what we can properly say in America. For many children, television has become a type of authority figure, such that what appears on television represents acceptable speech or it would not be on television. As a teacher and authority figure, you must decide what is appropriate for your classes.

Why Do We Have Word Etiquette?

Like other forms of etiquette, most children must learn the standards and conventions for communicating in American English. Why? Because conventional English is necessary to be functionally literate and to obtain many entry-level forms of employment in mainstream America. People without conventional language skills rarely reach high levels of achievement in economic, political, or social hierarchies. With conventional language skills, speakers are able to select which style is appropriate for a given occasion. Speakers limited to substandard language skills are stuck with a level of language (like one set of clothes) that will stigmatize them and limit their access to formal, restricted settings.

Sadly, many school children drop out of school or attend schools where they do not acquire proper communication skills. Other children and adults choose not to use conventional language and do not care about fitting into mainstream America. Even though some students resist conformity, both parents and teachers have a vested *and* shared interest in making sure children know the proper place of conventional language as well as the proper place of cursing language in contemporary society. Failing to teach students etiquette would violate one of the goals of modern education: to make students functional in the real world.

This discussion of etiquette is not to say that all types of dirty word usage must be completely eliminated but that children should know the consequences of dirty word use. Sexual harassment, discrimination, and violence in schools are serious problems that involve communication skills, and these language-related problems must be addressed by teachers and administrators.

The use of dirty words that results in insulting, harassing, or discriminating against students, thus denying victims a proper education, must be eliminated. Dirty words and insults have been with us for hundreds of years and cannot be eliminated completely from popular use (or from expressions of frustration or expressions of anger). The goal in this book is to make teachers more aware of why children use these words and what to do about it when they do.

What Are "Dirty" Words?

Parents tell their children not to use dirty words. Adults know that they are not supposed to use dirty words in front of their children. But just what is it that defines a word as dirty? It turns out that there are several types of dirty words. Some children may use one of these types but not other types.

A student's use of dirty words depends on the nature of the learning environment. Some parents may tolerate some forms of cursing in the home but not others, and their children head off to school thinking some forms of cursing are acceptable. Teachers need information about the different forms of dirty word usage and a warning about which forms present the most serious problems in school. An analysis of different categories of cursing begins in the next chapter.

Dirty Words, Generally Speaking

The phrase "talk dirty" is used in the title of this book to cover all sorts of cursing, swearing, and offensive word usage. We can also refer to the general use of dirty words as "cursing." The term "cursing" may be more helpful than the term "dirty words" because "cursing" is a more widely accepted term for the American public, although language experts might find it somewhat inexact. I use the term "cursing" to refer to several kinds of dirty word usage. The diversity of different kinds of cursing is what I mean by "different colors" in the chapter title.

In this book, we will consider how cursing is used at school and identify how the use of curse words affects both speakers and listeners. To start this study I list the categories of usage in which we place dirty words. Each usage or category has a different intention or function for the speaker. Immediately it will become obvious that the use of the term "cursing" or "dirty words" covers a number of different speaker intentions.

What Lies Ahead in This Book

The following nine chapters in Part One cover the different forms of dirty word usage that are most prevalent in school. I provide definitions, interpretations, and examples of each category to help you identify and compare different forms of cursing. All cursing is not equal. Each category of cursing presents a different set of problems and different solutions.

It is important for teachers and students to understand that all cursing is not equal, that there are differences in intentions and levels of offensiveness. Some forms are frequent and mildly offensive, but others are very offensive, problematic, and even illegal. In Parts Two and Three, I discuss the use of different types of cursing in the school context. In very practical terms I suggest how teachers can monitor and control problems with dirty words in Parts Four through Six.

Summary

- The term "dirty words" refers to several different types of language problems.

- Some types of dirty words are more problematic than others.

- Students must learn that dirty words are unacceptable in some contexts.

CHAPTER 2

Identifying Cursing

The intent of cursing, according to the standard definition, is to invoke harm on another person through the use of certain words or phrases. These phrases are imbued with a power granted to them mainly through religious or social institutions. In other words, certain institutions throughout history, like religion, have made a point to note that there exists in language a set of special words that are believed to be capable of harming listeners.

Curse words were restricted from usage by punishing the speaker for using them, which is another reason why the words seemed so powerful. These curse words thus obtained power to cause harm because physical and psychological punishments for using them were administered by those in authority. We have accepted that curse words are powerful and harmful because we were told they were powerful and were punished for using them.

Today, what Americans refer to as "cursing" or "cussing" (the person on the street uses "cuss" in non-specific meaning) bears some resemblance to curses and hexes of ancient times. However, it is doubtful that modern men and women think a curse brings about physical or mental harm, as our ancestors must have believed.

A religious curse may sound something like one of the following: "damn you," "goddamn you," "damn your hide," "to hell with you."

Cursing could also be non-religious but still wish harm to the target person, as in "Eat shit and die," "I wish you were dead, Mommy," "I hope you break your neck," or "You should rot in jail for that crime."

Children use cursing language against their schoolmates, siblings, parental figures, and the elderly when they are angry, frustrated, or upset.

Most American cursing amounts to fairly short, simple, and direct phrases that are conventionalized expressions of anger. Both the speaker and the target understand what is going on. The speaker knows that an act of cursing is intended and the listener knows when he or she is the target of the curse. Cursing occurs frequently as a response to frustration or provocation from another person. When we hear one child cursing a classmate, we have a pretty good idea that there is some tension and anger between the two. Cursing cannot be interpreted as a friendly act.

Children use cursing language against their schoolmates, siblings, parental figures, and the elderly (or anyone else who they perceive as different) at times when they are angry, aggressive, frustrated, taunted or upset. We hear curses on the playground, during athletic events, and when children become tired or upset. These episodes will most likely take the form of non-religious curses like those listed above. One goal for teachers is to retrain their students to express their anger without cursing (see chapter 23).

Summary

- "Cursing" refers to wishing harm on another person.

- Students curse when they are angry at or threatened by others.

CHAPTER 3

Identifying Profanity

The definition of profanity is based on the church's distinction between secular and religious speech. To be profane means to be secular or to behave in a manner that is outside the practice of religious standards or religious belief. To be profane means to be ignorant or intolerant of the guidelines of a particular religious order, but profanity is not a direct attack on the church or religion. An example of profanity would be the use of a word or phrase which seeks not to denigrate God, religion, or holy affairs *but* would be based more on one's ignorance of or indifference to these religious matters.

These profanities might sound something like one of the following: "Jesus H Christ, I'm hungry!", "For the love of Christ, get off the phone!", "He's a goddamned idiot," and "That's one hell of a law." These are common expressions employing religious terminology in a profane, secular, or indifferent manner.

Profanity is used very frequently in American speech, representing a misuse of religious terms and phrases. As a category of dirty word usage, it represents about half of all the questionable language in television and motion picture content that children may hear. Every form of our media is filled with profanity. Profanities appear almost every day in newspaper comic strips read by children. Profanities can be heard by children every day on the radio.

Through frequent usage, most of us have become desensitized to profanity. We hear profanity so frequently that we stop listening to it and fail to realize just how frequently it occurs. While profanity

We hear profanity so frequently that we stop listening to it and fail to realize just how frequently it occurs.

represents one of the milder forms of swearing today, it still may be very upsetting to some religious people. Unfortunately, it does not look like the conversational use of profanity will slow down.

Profanity has been on the increase since World War II, and there is no reason to believe its usage will decrease in the future. The pervasiveness of profanity in our media gives consumers the impression that it is acceptable. Religious figures and children's advocacy groups have been unable to stop the trend toward the widespread use of profane speech.

Summary

- "Profanity" refers to ignorance or indifference to religious matters.

- It occurs very frequently in American society.

- Relative to more offensive obscenities, it is mildly offensive.

CHAPTER 4

Identifying Blasphemy

Ablasphemy is a direct attack on religion or religious doctrine. Because it also relies on religious reference, blasphemy is related to, but not the same as, profanity. A common confusion among speakers of English is to assume that profanity and blasphemy mean the same thing. When we examine the intent of each speech form, we see that profanity and blasphemy are different. The distinction is based on the intention of the speaker. Profane speakers mean no harm but blasphemers do. Blasphemers intend to target the church with their speech.

While profanity is related to the secular indifference to religion, blasphemy aims directly at the church and religious figures. These verbal assaults would take the form of using the Lord's name in vain, cursing the deities, or showing intentional disrespect for religion and religious figures or church doctrine.

As organized religions have lost much of their power over the everyday life of twentieth-century Americans, blasphemy has lost its impact as an insult. The church can no longer punish blasphemers in America as it once did. However, while these expressions are particularly offensive to the very devout, they may be regarded as humorous to non-believers. Some examples are "Screw the church!" "To hell with what it says in the Bible!" "Father O'Reilly can kiss my ass!" "The church can stick their new fund drive!"

In the past, blasphemy in America was punishable by death or excommunication. Some foreign countries still treat blasphemy very

Blasphemy has lost its power to offend the average American, but there are still some locations within the United States, some extremely devout communities, where blasphemy is unacceptable.

seriously and may punish blasphemers with imprisonment or even death. Today, however, blasphemy has lost its power to offend the average American, but there are still some locations within the United States, some extremely devout communities, where blasphemy is unacceptable. These religious communities may be less tolerant of blasphemy, and the rural school districts therein may have more conservative standards and values compared to large, multi-cultural urban school districts.

Church members in some religions may be informed and cautioned about the blasphemous content of questionable books, television programs, or motion pictures. Newsletters, radio and television broadcasts, and movie guides may recommend that members and children not read the offensive books or view the offensive films. Some religious values end up in the school.

A community's religious values regarding language may be reflected in school policies. In some religious communities, sex talk, sex education, profane speech on campus, and clothing with vulgar words may be restricted on school grounds. Blasphemy may be one type of restricted language.

Summary

- Blasphemy is an attack on religion and religious figures.
- It is mildly offensive but more offensive than profanity.
- Like profanity, blasphemy occurs frequently in everyday speech.

CHAPTER 5

Identifying Obscenity

Obscenity is defined by law. Early in American history, our courts sought to restrict speech which was thought capable of corrupting and depraving the minds of young children. Such speech was thought to represent a prurient or lascivious interest in sexual matters. United States obscenity laws changed following Supreme Court rulings between 1950 and 1970. Current obscenity laws focus on community standards, artistic values, and applicable state and federal rulings.

The person on the street uses the term "obscene" too casually (and incorrectly). "Obscenity" is clearly a legal term, defined through legal decisions. Only within a court of law can a book, movie, or recording be judged to be obscene. The function of obscenity laws is to protect listeners and viewers from exposure to offensive speech.

In American society, we have free speech, but some types of speech, which are defined or outlined by the law, can be controlled and restricted. We can speak as we choose but only within reason and the law. Obscene speech means unprotected speech; unprotected speech is not free but subject to the restrictions of a governing (federal, state, or local government) body.

Sometimes obscenity is mistakenly confused with a related notion of language "taboos." While the notion of taboo restricts or inhibits what *speakers* say, obscenity functions to protect *listeners* from harmful language. Obscenity laws control the content of books and audio and video broadcasts to protect the audience while taboos in a society control the content of speakers' sentences to protect the speaker.

In American English, obscenities are pointedly sexual in nature.

In American English, obscenities are pointedly sexual in nature. They do not necessarily have to be so. For example, it could be decided that words that depict physical violence such as "kill," "rape" or "murder" are more dangerous than sexual terms. But Americans are most fearful of sex. It is the sex act, sexual deviation, and related sexual imagery that have been deemed by the courts to be so offensive that they cannot be freely uttered.

Obscene words are considered the most offensive and are rarely, if ever, used in public media. Some words that gain universal restriction are "fuck," "twat," "prick," "motherfucker," "cocksucker," "cunt," or "tits."

The obscene word "fuck," although restricted in media, is one of the most frequently recorded dirty words in public, especially when it is used as an expletive, a brief emotional outburst of anger.

Indecent Speech

A broader and less offensive category of restricted speech is defined as indecent speech, based on court rulings and Federal Communication Commission standards. The media use the term "indecency" or "indecent language" to restrict or control the content of radio, television, or cable presentations. Indecent speech includes milder obscenities and vulgar or crude references to body products and body functions through euphemisms or indirect references. For example, describing someone urinating or defecating in detailed terms would be defined as indecent but not obscene.

Technically, what is indecent is determined by those who monitor and control media content. Factors also influence the acceptability of the language therein. The time of the broadcast is one example (late at night is fine). The fact that some language has been banned from the public airwaves does not mean that it is obscene. The category of indecent speech was defined in order to protect children from adult words and concepts in mass media daytime programming. Most recently these indecency rulings have focused on children's television and "shock radio" broadcasts.

Obscenity is the most offensive category of speech to be dealt with by parents and teachers. Because it is defined by the outcomes of legal decisions, it may be easier than other types of dirty words to identify and restrict. Unfortunately for teachers, obscenities are becoming commonplace in the colloquial speech of children. You will hear them most commonly when children are angry. Obscenity is frequently used in adolescents' colloquial speech.

Summary

- Obscenity is a legal concept.
- It is based on sexual matters and sexual deviance.
- Obscenity is the most offensive type of cursing in American English.

CHAPTER 6

Identifying Sexual Harassment

Like obscenity, sexual harassment is a legal term and has been defined by the federal government. What constitutes "verbal sexual harassment" within a school setting will develop and evolve through federal and state legal decisions as the definition of obscenity did. Administrators and teachers have to keep up with court rulings in harassment cases to know how sexual harassment is defined. Sexual harassment is a relatively new concept, and each new case refines of the term.

At this point, we know that sexual harassment is based on unwanted sexual remarks, dirty jokes, references to one's appearance, or sexual behavior. The notion of verbal sexual harassment includes public speech, restroom graffiti, written comments on clothing, and oral remarks made at school or during trips to and from school. Harassment includes behaviors and speech that occur during school, after school, and off campus.

What constitutes sexual harassment? The legal definition seems quite specific but it is not. According to the EEOC Rules and Regulations (U.S. Equal Employment Opportunity Commission 1980), it is:

> Unwelcome sexual advances, requests for sexual favors, and other verbal or physical conduct of a sexual nature constitute unlawful sexual harassment when (a) submission to such conduct is made either explicitly or implicitly a term or condition of an individual's employment, (b) submission to or rejection of such conduct by an individual is used as the basis for employment

Dealing with sexual harassment is very serious business and you must know what it is and how to deal with it, directly and appropriately.

decisions affecting such individual, or (c) such conduct has the purpose or effect of unreasonably interfering with an individual's work performance or creating an intimidating, hostile, or offensive working environment. An employer is responsible for sexual harassment by its agents or supervisory employees regardless of whether the employer knew or should have known of their occurrence. An employer is responsible for acts of sexual harassment in the workplace committed by "nonsupervisory employees" where the employer knows or should have known of the conduct and no immediate and appropriate corrective action was taken.

A competent school system should have one person on the staff who keeps others appraised of changes in the laws and current court cases involving harassment at school. These court updates keep teachers knowledgeable about what types of language would constitute sexual harassment. The school should also have a person to register and respond to complaints of sexual harassment, generally someone working in the personnel office.

Sexual harassment claims can be based on episodes involving comments about the way someone looks; comments about one's sexual behavior, sexual looseness, or sexual preferences; references to body parts; references that denigrate a person based on gender ("bitch," "little woman," "honey," "chick," "broad," or "girlie"); or dirty jokes told to people who do not want to hear them. These sexual references and comments are those that can create a hostile working environment and diminish the effectiveness of one's work.

Dealing with sexual harassment is serious business and you must know what it is and how to deal with it, directly and appropriately.

Summary

- Sexual harassment refers to unwanted sexual remarks, dirty jokes, and references to one's sexual behavior or appearance.

- It is increasingly problematic in schools, especially from boys.

- Sexual harassment is clearly unacceptable speech and must be addressed by the staff.

CHAPTER 7

Identifying Vulgar Language

Vulgarity" refers to the language of the common person, "the person in the street." It is unsophisticated, raw, suggestive, crude, unsocialized, uneducated, or uncivilized speech. "Vulgar" does not mean "bad," nor does it mean "obscene." Using vulgarities does not serve any unique language function. Use of vulgar language fulfills normal communication demands within common human discourse. The problem with vulgarity is that these words are inappropriate in some social settings. Vulgar words are low on the formality and acceptability scale; they are the "dirty laundry" of the human vocabulary.

The recognition of vulgarity is a value judgment placed on working-class language by the upper classes. As such, the designation represents a form of linguistic snobbery. Consider the following example. After the Normans invaded England in 1066, the French language was identified as the official language to be used in business, religious, and legal affairs. To use Anglo-Saxon terms was to be vulgar or common. During the Victorian era, society again returned to a period of stigmatizing language considered crude or vulgar when it was suggested that speakers call a chicken breast "white meat" and a chicken leg "dark meat" because "leg" and "breast" were considered suggestive at the time.

Throughout history, lower-class slang and vulgar language have appeared in colloquial speech while the lower classes have acquired and used prestigious language spoken by the upper class. Even as the lower class gains the use of more standard language terms, the upper class through social mobility and education continues to define

To be vulgar is to be common, not necessarily bad or evil.

the more prestigious lexicon. To be vulgar is to be common, not necessarily bad or evil. Vulgarity survived all attempts to censor, suppress, or eradicate it by those with power and prestige.

A vulgarity is not necessarily obscene or taboo but usually reflects the crudeness of street language. The use of vulgarity has direct implications for educators because it has a limited place in classroom communication. Hearing students overuse vulgar language gives the listener the impression that the speakers lack formal education, etiquette, or refinement. Some words and phrases considered vulgar today are: "snot," "bloody," "up yours," "booger," "boobs," "slut," "piss," "crap," "kiss my ass," "snatch," "on the rag," "puke," "douche bag," "knockers," "pecker," and "jugs."

Whether we will hear vulgar terms like those above depends on the social groups with which we interact. Using vulgarity is still a marker of social status for many Americans. Eliminating vulgarities amongst children would seem a worthy goal to many. Some communities may produce more vulgarities than others, depending on prevailing social, intellectual, and economic conditions and values operating in the community. Reactions to vulgarity, as to whether it is "proper" or not, depend on one's social-economic status.

Address educational goals and explain community values when discussing the topic of vulgarity with students. In communities riddled with poverty, unemployment, and high dropout rates, overcoming vulgar speech may be a daunting task. Parents and other adults in poor communities may use vulgarity in almost all settings. Young school students in such communities need good role models for alternative ways of expressing ideas. Tell students that in order to sound like an educated person and to be able to communicate with educated speakers and authority figures (ministers, doctors, and police officers), vulgarity should be suppressed. Teach students that vulgar language is inappropriate for certain formal social contexts such as classroom discussions, written assignments, public debate, and communicating on the job.

Summary

- Vulgarity refers to the mildly offensive language of common people.

- Vulgarity is generally perceived as undereducated or illiterate speech.

- Vulgarity is inappropriate for classroom communication.

CHAPTER 8

Identifying Insults,
Name Calling, and Ethnic Slurs

Insults and slurs are verbal attacks, or put downs, on other people. These words are spoken with intent to harm, demean, or denigrate the listener. Merely saying these words to another person is an insult to him or her. Insults and slurs do not gain their power to offend from religious circles. Instead, an insulting word's power to offend is defined and specified by social rules learned "on the street" and in social interaction. Whatever constitutes an insulting word and its degree of offensiveness is highly conventionalized and passed down from generation to generation. Children learn early in life the words "nigger" and "bitch" because they observe other speakers using these insults to offend people.

Insults gain their impact by denoting real or imagined negative characteristics of a target or victim. Names are given the status or power to be insulting through social recognition as insults and through the repeated use as insults. Slurs may be racial, ethnic, or social in nature. The use of slurs may indicate racial stereotyping or prejudice on the part of a speaker.

Insults, slurs, and name calling denote the physical, mental, or psychological qualities of the victim. Insults are commonly heard on the school playground and during active play. Both insults and names function to hurt a target by the mere use of words which have conditioned emotional meanings (words which are negative and hurtful).

This language usually indicates a lack of respect for others on the part of the speaker.

The use of insults reflects the way speakers view other groups of people. Insults used in early childhood are concrete and refer to visible differences. "Fatty" is one example. But as children grow older and can think about people in a more abstract way, the words they use to insult peers become more abstract, reflecting greater social sophistication and less reliance on physical or visible differences. "Welfare cheat" is an example. Therefore, adult insults differ from what children use as insults but generally are restricted to a few categories of thought. Some common insults use animal imagery: "pig," "dog," "bitch," "son of a bitch," "jackass," and "sow." Some are based on perceived social deviations: "whore," "sissy," "tomboy," "slut," "bastard," "homo," "fag," and "dyke."

Children's name calling and insults are commonly based on perceived abnormal physical, psychological, or social characteristics. These may seem childish when used by adults, but they do set the stage for adult-level name calling and stereotyping. Consider the following: "fatty," "freckles," "bubble butt," "booger nose," "four eyes," "spaz," "brain," "retard," "dumb," "weirdo," "blabber mouth," "fag," "liar," "tattle tale," "cry baby," "fairy," "old fart," and "wimp."

Ethnic and Racial Slurs

Most readers are familiar with the many ethnic and racial slurs. These are spoken derogatorily to members of those groups: "honky," "nazi," "white trash," "redneck," "dago," "spic," "nigger," "wop," "kike," "chink," "frog," "wet back," "gook," "slope," "mick," "grease ball," "pollack," "nip," "Uncle Tom," "yid," "guinea," "goy," "slant-eyed," "PR," "hebe," and "greaser."

Some terms are based on food preferences: "chili chaser," "spaghetti bender," "beaner," "mackerel snapper," "kraut," and "limey."

Some terms are based on ethnic customs or religion: "towel head," "bead squeezer," "Christ killer," "Bible Belter," "holy roller," and "fish eater."

Each of these insults and slurs generally is intended to hurt the listener. These terms are used by members on an in-group to insult members of an out-group. Sometimes these groups compete for limited resources within a community and tensions arise. Lower status groups become the targets of scapegoating and frustration.

Some conventional insults, such as "nigger" and "pig," referring to the police, can become fighting words used to trigger or escalate aggression between different group members. Members of an ethnic group, such as African Americans on the other hand, can use the insulting term "nigger" within their group as terms of endearment or in joking with each other. When non-African Americans use the same term, the speakers will be viewed as prejudiced rather than endearing. This in-group versus out-group difference in usage occurs for many different groups.

It is becoming increasingly clear that some types of insults and slurs cannot be tolerated in schools. Recent rulings by state courts give students the right to bring lawsuits against teachers and students for speech used as a form of sexual harassment. In addition, fighting words and speech-based racial discrimination can be restricted at school. These language restrictions apply to clothing, nonverbal gestures, graffiti, or signs at school as well as spoken words. Teachers should be aware of the laws that have been passed to achieve equality and eliminate discrimination.

- Title VII of the Civil Rights Bill prohibits discrimination based on race, color, national origin, or gender.

- Title IX of the 1972 Education Amendment prohibits denial of full participation in all educational programs and activities based on gender.

Teachers who want to eliminate racial slurs, ethnic jokes, and insults should instruct their students that this language usually indicates a lack of respect for others on the part of the speaker and that racial insults underlie prejudiced attitudes. These words reduce victims to the level of stereotypes based only on superficial characteristics and may be indicative of a speaker's intolerance. The golden rule is a great way to get the point across and instill mutual respect.

While we have been dealing with racial and ethnic differences for decades, we are just beginning to eliminate many of the sexist remarks from our workplace and schools, which include both written and oral communication in classrooms. Dealing with gender-related insults will need more attention from educators in the future.

Summary

- Insults, name calling, and racial slurs denote real or imagined differences between victims and speakers.

- They may represent unacceptable forms of discrimination.

- They may cause an escalation of violence if uncontrolled at school.

CHAPTER 9

Identifying Scatological Language

Scatological references are among the first words that children hear and use when they are being toilet trained. "Scatology" refers to words used to describe body products and elimination. Americans have a great penchant for coining childish terms for body products and elimination rather than using formal or clinical terms. Scatological insults are common among children. Some examples are: "poo poo," "kaka," "poop," "turd," "crap," "shit," "pee pee," "shit ass," "shit for brains," "piss," "piss pot," "piss off," and "fart." The terms children say are usually different than those adults would pick for the same referent. Some say only a vulgar person would use scatological terms when a more refined euphemism or technical term could be substituted.

These scatological references represent a mild form of dirty language usage that can be eliminated by parents who should avoid them in the first place. Regardless of what parents do, children will still be exposed to this level of communication in popular entertainment and in peer interactions at school and in the neighborhood.

Teachers should deal with scatology as they do with vulgar language and tell students that these terms are inappropriate for formal social settings. Using such language indicates that the speaker is childish, undereducated, and lacks social awareness about formal language customs such as using clinical terms for body parts, products, and processes.

Scatological references are considered indecent speech in the realm of radio and television broadcasting. Even though scatological

Scatological references are about feces and elimination.

references commonly appear in movies for children and in popular music, presenting such material during daytime programming would not be suitable. Students who want to pursue a career in media or public communication must have alternative, appropriate language. The fact that scatology is restricted in public discourse indicates that it is an inappropriate form of expression; therefore, it should be censored in classrooms and educational communications.

Summary

- Scatology is based on feces and elimination.

- It is mildly offensive and regarded as childish speech.

CHAPTER 10

Identifying Slang

Slang is a special vocabulary that is created within certain social groups (teenagers, musicians, soldiers, physicians, drug users, or athletes) in order to simplify communication and solidify the members of the group. The slang code serves to identify members of the subculture while misuse or ignorance of the correct slang terms identifies a speaker as a non-member. Group identification through a common language is especially important in illegal transactions like drug dealing and prostitution. Using slang inappropriately would identify the speaker as a non-member of the in-group.

A slang word ("dis") may develop through simplifying or abbreviating wordy or complex notions ("disrespect"). Slang words may also provide a more specific reference, for example, to a specific drug name ("speed" or "black beauty") as opposed to the scientific or conventional name that non-group members use ("amphetamine").

Slang is the province of children and teenagers. Children create, accept, and thrive on slang because the use of slang helps differentiate and separate children from adults and authority figures. Slang allows children to develop an identity of their own. Frequently used slang words expand beyond the subculture that created them. Sometimes slang terms ("ripped off") become so popular and widespread that they are used in mainstream communications, putting pressure on subgroup members to invent a new code. Other slang terms, like the use of "shit" to mean "heroin," are too offensive to the general public and are never integrated into standard dialects.

Children create, accept, and thrive on slang because the use of slang helps differentiate and separate children from adults and authority

Slang words are constantly generated and renewed. Older terms become marked as obsolete and fall from usage. If a speaker uses obsolete slang, he or she would be regarded as being out of touch. Slang usage is easily observed among teenagers, musicians, athletes, soldiers, drug users, gang members, prostitutes, athletes, and other cultural subgroups. Slang terms are words like the following: "pimp," "cherry," "dweeb," "ho," "bennies," "mid-term," "john," "dis," "cupcakes," "s-o-s," "jelly roll," "skank," "mack daddy," "wanker," "slammin'," "homie," "OG," "9 mm," "pipe," "crack," and "jock."

The slang we are interested in is that which is most offensive within the school context such as "ho," "buttwipe," "asswipe," "dipshit," "booty snatcher," "dickwad," or "douche bag." The distinction between other dirty word categories and slang is not always clear. Slang draws offensive references from popular culture and popular media that may also overlap other semantic categories. What makes them slang is that they are used within groups of youthful speakers for a brief period of time to be replaced later by new words when the old ones become passé.

Slang and jargon will always be a part of American culture and communication. Parents and teachers will continually be plagued with it. The stratification of American culture by profession, income, race, and age factors guarantees that groups will develop special language to be used among in-group members. Children, especially teenagers, will create and destroy language to suit their own needs to differentiate themselves from adults.

American popular culture in the form of music, film, and literature is the engine that drives the creation of slang. The more children interact with different groups or subgroups that generate and perpetuate the use of slang the more likely slang will appear in their speech.

Parents, teachers, and caregivers should make an attempt to keep up with the jargon that children use by watching and listening to their children's entertainment. In some cases, the use of drug terms, for example, indicate that children have had contact with a drug culture at school or in the community. If you do not know the jargon, you will not know what is "going down." In the reference section of a good library, there will be several books on the topic. Other resources would be teenagers' popular magazines, books, and newspapers.

Summary

- Slang is developed by subgroups to identify and solidify in-group members.

- It helps children differentiate themselves from adults and others.

- Slang is widespread in popular culture and only mildly offensive.

- It should be familiar to teachers who examine children's media.

PART TWO

Identifying
Your Values

CHAPTER 11

Are There National Language Values?

We have restrictions on public speech that apply across the nation. These restrictions are derived from legal decisions and media or business standards. With the status of nationwide standards and laws, such restrictions on language must be incorporated into a school's value system.

Americans also have national language values (or standards) based on convention and common sense. American English has been influenced by a wide variety of languages brought to this country by immigrants with very different ethnic and religious beliefs. The need to be understood, to be polite, to influence others and to achieve goals with language impels speakers to adopt common sense conventions; taking turns within a conversation and not talking for too long are two examples. Certainly those language values that are derived from federal court decisions must be of primary importance for teachers, with common sense and conventional values not far behind.

The national language standards proscribed for mass media and mass communication are set by policy makers within the media to comply with federal laws. Media language standards are also results of the influence of pressure groups who complain about media content. Other restrictions on language govern conduct and speech in public places, language in telephone conversations, and the nature

National labor standards and federal laws restrict the speech that can be used in schools across the country.

of formal business communication. These restrictions may be imposed on spoken, written, electronic, and graphic forms of speech. Sources of national language values are discussed below.

Federal Court Decisions

Teachers and school administrators must obey the law of the land. While the First Amendment grants freedom of speech, the Supreme Court has ruled that some types of speech are not protected. Obscenity (see chapter 5), fighting words (personally provocative speech that leads to immediate violence), words which pose imminent danger (yelling "fire" in a crowded theater), defamation, slander, or libel (making damaging, false statements about a person in writing or orally), and verbal sexual harassment (see chapter 6) are good examples of speech that is restricted in public. Obviously, federal laws that govern communication practices in public schools must be addressed in school policies.

New Laws

After a court has handed down a ruling about speech, it takes time for businesses and communities to react to and adopt the new standards. Some communities may adopt even more stringent standards than are outlined in federal court rulings. Restrictive community standards have been used to control what language can appear on bumper stickers, what kinds of tee shirts patrons can wear to museums, and what people can say in public places.

Teachers' communications at school are directly affected by laws regarding harassment, discrimination, and obscenity. National obscenity laws apply to extremely offensive language, and obscene language is defined by courts. However, the definition of sexual harassment is not simple. The language of harassment may be very subtle and include references to the way people look, jokes of a sexual nature, and comments about sexual behavior. Different forms of cursing (harassment, discrimination, and obscenity) were discussed in Part One.

Federal courts have ruled that schools are responsible for upholding obscenity and harassment standards and that schools can be found negligent and assessed damages in cases when the school's staff allowed students to be harassed. Therefore, schools must have explicit policies that address and conform to national language standards. Language and behavior values and regulations must be taught to and discussed with students from time to time.

Mass Communication

Print and electronic media must follow industry standards and federal court rulings. Most newspapers, magazines, and printed materials omit obscenities and even indecent speech. Broadcasters, owners, and editors are responsible for media content, and they are subject to pressure groups and court decisions. Television and motion pictures are policed on a national basis for offensive content through rating systems and viewer response.

Educators who use popular media in classroom presentations (films, music, and magazines) must determine if the content of the presentation is appropriate for the intended audience. For example, showing movies rated R or NC-17 to teenagers would prove problematic for most schools. Even though a popular film or book is acceptable for the American public, these materials require close scrutiny on campus.

Any school teacher or student who participates in or creates media to be consumed by the general public has to follow media standards and restrictions. These are most likely to occur with printed newspapers and radio or television productions that are created by and for the school population.

Recently, the offensive language appearing in e-mail communications and campus computer network bulletin boards has come under scrutiny. Offensive language emerges in every new medium and within every new technological improvement in communication. However, the current communication laws and standards regarding the use of offensive language in emerging technology will continue to evolve but lag behind innovation. Teachers and administrators now need to monitor the use of dirty words in school computer communications.

Computer communication has been implicated in recent court rulings regarding sexual harassment. One case in California involved a group of male college students who posted offensive descriptions and evaluations of women on their campus. The courts are just beginning to define and outline restrictions on speech on computer networks. One parameter that needs to be addressed in computer communication is whether private computer messages among users are private speech or whether they are a form sexual harassment. Schools that allow students to communicate with each other with computers, either interactively on-line or through computer bulletin boards, should make sure that students and teachers are not breaking any laws (harassment, discrimination, or slander) when they send messages via computers.

Workplace Settings and the Business World

Teachers and students interact in a school setting or workplace that is equivalent to other workplace settings in America. The school as a workplace comes with certain established rights and responsibilities. Students should learn how to communicate in a workplace since they are going to end up in a workplace following graduation. Students should learn that communication in the workplace is sanctioned by the federal courts and other times by labor law and management practices. Recent Supreme Court rulings on sexual harassment have focused on what managers have said to workers.

Businesses and industries who do business in global and national markets usually hire people who speak standard or conventional English. The use of obscenity, slang, or taboo speech in public business transactions is inappropriate and subject to restrictions based on conventional standards. Of course, teachers' and students' conversations in private settings are not so restricted. But in general, most business-like transactions and formal communications are subject to a high level of language etiquette. Students should learn to conform to language standards at school in preparation for communicating effectively in the American workplace.

It should also be noted that restrictions on teacher-student communications are not limited only to that speech which is used in the classroom. Confrontations among students and teachers in public places cannot occur as if there were no predetermined relationship between the two parties. Thus, students cannot verbally assault teachers in the local shopping mall without repercussions at school. Similarly, intimate teacher-student relationships off campus are rarely interpreted as freely occurring relationships since both parties must acknowledge a prior student-teacher relationship established at school. In reality, students are rarely held to language standards as high as teachers' classroom language standards. While teachers are subject to dismissal for inappropriate language, students do not face such harsh consequences.

Summary

National labor standards and federal laws restrict the speech that can be used in schools across the country. Teachers must obey these laws and students preparing to enter the workplace upon reaching adulthood have to follow the same laws. The school campus is "the real world" and those working in it have to communicate according to the rules. Media used on campus, like newspapers, magazines, radio, television, motion pictures, and computer-based communications, must conform to media standards and applicable federal and state laws.

CHAPTER 12

Are There Regional Language Values?

Speakers living in different parts of the country have different standards for defining appropriate language. These regional standards are derived from the ethnic and religious backgrounds of those who settled and are living in a region. Regional customs and preferences regarding language are incorporated in speakers' value systems to varying degrees, depending on how closely one identifies with the region.

Unfortunately, many of our impressions about the way Americans speak and the values they cherish come from the media we consume. Most of the media we consume comes from either New York or Los Angeles, not from less populous regions of the country. The smaller, less mainstream, and eccentric communities are ignored. The big city bias coverage in our media engenders a distorted view of American English and glosses over regional differences in language use. Regional dialects are heard on local broadcasts but only rarely on the national level.

Students from large metropolitan areas are more likely to use offensive street language than students raised in rural America.

The Basis for Regional Differences

Social-Ethnic Differences

Regional differences are derived from the mix of ethnic cultures who inhabit a geographic area. Communities with one dominant ethnic group may have fairly uniform standards. Consider the Amish in Pennsylvania and Ohio or the Polish, Italian, Chinese, Japanese, and Russian ghettos in large cities where foreign languages are accustomed to the exclusion of English. Metropolitan communities with diverse cultures have different values and conflicting language values. One ethnic group within a diverse community may use profanities freely while another strictly avoids irreligious and profane speech. Ethnic differences also become the source of insults and name calling.

Dialects

Americans have a tendency to discriminate against people with dialects they perceive to be less cultured than their own regional dialect. One of the most obvious differences is based on northern versus southern dialects. Another difference occurs when we can identify those who speak with foreign dialects and accents. Dialect patterns, word choice, and prestige dialects differ from state to state, region to region, and even within communities of a large city. Speakers who aspire to climb the social ladder try to emulate speech patterns of prestige groups, usually well-educated and rich people.

Those speakers who are unable or unwilling to speak conventional or prestige dialects value conventional speech patterns less than those who do value prestige patterns. Such regional dialect patterns may be a source of tension among your students, especially in schools with students from diverse and competing ethnic backgrounds. For example, recent Mexican student immigrants in Southern California find group solidarity and security by retaining their native language at school. Long-time, non-immigrant resident students interpret the use of the Spanish language negatively. Recent immigrants are the target of insults because they do not speak English well. As a result, teachers have to remain open-minded about dialect differences and should not stigmatize students from one population because of the way they speak. Sometimes teachers inadvertently denigrate speakers of different dialects through hypercorrection, further supporting student prejudice against differences.

Big Cities and Small Towns

Those who travel around the country probably have heard much more dirty language in big cities than small towns. New York City, Washington, DC, Boston, Chicago, Los Angeles, and San Francisco are good examples of big cities where there is plenty of cursing on the street. Speakers in large metropolitan areas adopt more relaxed (or liberal) personal language standards because the community does not enforce language restrictions and because much of their communication is anonymous or impersonal. People move about more quickly on the street and in traffic, giving little opportunity for retaliation or retribution for the use of cursing language.

Language usage is more restrictive in small-town America. Students from large metropolitan areas are more likely to use offensive street language than students raised in rural America. City children who move to rural areas may be perceived as rude and out-of-place by the local students. For example, teachers in western Massachusetts see dialect conflicts frequently involving Boston-area students who relocate to the rural western part of the state. Both city and small town students feel uncomfortable with the other group's language and clothing styles. Language and dialect differences become a source of insults between small-town and big-city students.

Small towns and religious communities across the country are less likely than big cities to tolerate obscenities in public. Speakers are less anonymous, parents are more vigilant, and sanctions on misconduct are more probable. School children raised in small rural areas grow up with a much less elaborate knowledge of words related to drugs, sexual behavior, and popular culture relative to children raised in urban areas, who hear more offensive language in their communities on a daily basis. As an example, consider that within the Bible Belt and small-town America, one sees with regularity signs prohibiting the use of foul language in restaurants, taverns, retail stores, and public facilities.

In general, the smaller the region we inhabit, the more likely we are to find consensus about what language is acceptable in the region. Teachers and students in small towns face more restrictions than teachers and students in urban areas. However, in all fairness to the topic of language values, dirty language usage may be of minor importance in large city schools which are plagued by violence, unemployment, drug use, and social unrest.

Reference Material on Regional Dialects

Regional differences in language are covered in the *Dictionary of American Regional English*, available in many large libraries. This book describes the slang and insult terms (among other lexical differences for food, animals, and so forth) that are unique to a particular region of the country. There is a videotape entitled *American Tongues* that provides a valuable analysis of dialect differences that are a source of friction. This video may be a resource for faculty sensitization training on the issue of regional language differences. Once teachers and students are receptive to the notion of language differences, they can more readily discuss what words and dialects they like and do not like.

Summary

Regional language values develop from social-ethnic differences, local dialects, prestige dialects, and the number of people in a geographic region. Small towns with homogeneous populations exhibit more agreement about language values relative to large multi-ethnic cities.

CHAPTER 13

Are There Cultural and Ethnic Language Values?

Teachers must be attentive to the cultural backgrounds of their students and the diversity of ethnic groups within the school district. Cultural, economic, and ethnic differences are sources of racial and ethnic slurs in every community. Each student comes to school with a different set of values depending on the beliefs of his or her parents and family. The differences in values form a basis for group identification.

Every school district has prestige groups which define the requirements for in-group membership and relegate undesirable outsiders to non-prestige or out-groups. Children perceived as different tend to get picked on, teased, and made fun of. Students use actual and perceived ethnic and social differences in neighborhoods, food preferences, income, race, occupation, religious practices, and gender as sources of name calling and insulting. These ethnic insults may be perceived as more insulting than obscenities for some children. The use of ethnic or racial slurs ("fighting words") may lead directly to violence for some students.

In large cities, students may belong to youth gangs (Crips or Bloods) that are established on the basis of racial background (African Americans), membership in a minority group (Mexicans), or local geographic neighborhoods (turf or 'hood). Some students may be attracted to these gangs and emulate gang members' slang. Gang

Teachers and administrators should have a working knowledge of the words, signs, and gestures that are offensive to their students.

members are very sensitive to name calling and insulting language derived from cultural and ethnic differences, and they retaliate against name calling and disrespectful behavior. These ethnic differences expressed in insulting language are not limited to language but also include gang signs, colors, dress styles, jewelry, icons, nonverbal gestures, and graffiti.

Summary

Teachers and administrators should have a working knowledge of the words, signs, and gestures that are offensive to their students. Teachers may need instruction in cultural differences or diversity training by bilingual counselors. Perhaps a local youth advocate or police gang patrol officer can instruct the faculty on more problematic language issues (signs, gestures, and graffiti). Teachers can also maintain a pipeline of information with each other to stay aware of new language and gestures.

CHAPTER 14

Are There Pertinent Religious Language Values?

Teachers should realize that some religious practices restrict language. Many schools may have a diverse population with different ethnic and religious affiliations while other private schools may have a fairly homogeneous population, all practicing one religion. Certainly, religious references have been used as insults for centuries, and the nature of these insults would depend on the in-groups and out-groups in question.

Many devout speakers have restrictions on the use of language about sexual references and references which are classified as profanity or blasphemy (see Part One). Offensive sexual terms and references for the devout could be forbidden in all contexts, including schools. Parents and older family members may be more concerned with these religious values than young children. On the other hand, some parents teach their children to be prejudiced against those who practice different religions, resulting in discriminatory beliefs and insulting language based on church affiliation.

Discriminatory and derogatory attitudes manifest themselves in insults, racial slurs, and name calling. Virtually every form of religion has been the target of insulting language. These insults may be based on religious references and ethnic origin ("bead squeezer," "Jew," "dago," "Hebe," "mackerel snapper," "yid," "kike," "holy roller," "Christ-killer," "Bible Belter," "Muslim," "camel jockey," and "towel

What religious tensions exist in your community depends on the mix of religions and each religion's social-economic impact.

head"). Although there appears to be a great deal of religious tolerance in America, Catholics and other Christian denominations, Jews, Buddhists, and Muslims have been the target of hate crimes throughout our history. What religious tensions exist in your community depends on the mix of religions and each religion's social-economic impact.

The local papers and Yellow Pages would provide some information to a teacher about the scope and diversity of different religious groups in the community. Principals and counselors may also provide demographic data about students and their families. This information may be of particular interest to teachers in communities that have experienced a recent influx of immigrants or newcomers.

We must realize that religious conflict throughout the world may increase tension in the community. Events in Northern Ireland, Africa, China, Mexico, Haiti, Cuba, Palestine, Israel, South Los Angeles, Miami, Brooklyn, Iraq, Memphis, Korea, Russia or England may incite different groups of students in big city schools. Large metropolitan school districts, where many different religions are practiced, experience more difficulty with religious conflicts than smaller, less religiously diverse communities.

Summary

Religious customs and differences continue to be the source of insulting language when there is social-economic disparity between religious groups within a school district. Teachers should be aware that some students may be more sensitive and more devout than others and that language values differ across religious groups.

CHAPTER 15

What Are My Students' Language Values?

When we listen to students speaking, we hear a wide range of offensiveness in their colloquial speech. Some references that would not offend an emotionally secure adult might prove to be very devastating to an oversensitive child such as a reference to physical appearance ("fatty") or mental ability ("stupid"). Each of us has a different threshold for insults. Some students have been taught by parents or peers that to suffer an insult without retaliation is a sign of weakness. These students have been taught to retaliate against the people who insult them. Other students have been taught to turn the other cheek or to remember the childhood saying, "Sticks and stones...." Teachers have to figure out the nature and depth of each individual student's values and the values supported by different student reference groups by paying attention to what their students say to each other.

Students frequently use speech styles and knowledge of slang to differentiate themselves from others. Students develop their own vocabulary in order to identify with their peers and distance themselves from parents, adults, or groups of students perceived as outsiders. Selective vocabulary and group identification are natural phenomena and cannot be changed by teacher strategies.

Students in middle schools are likely to imitate the speech patterns and vocabulary of those they admire in their neighborhoods

You do not have to speak the language your students speak but you do have to know what students are talking about in your classroom.

and in popular culture. Teachers may not hear the nuances of slang in formal classroom discussions. Often what teachers hear in the classroom is more conventional than what students say freely on the playground where different attitudes are more likely to be contested. This is to say that teachers cannot hear all of the slang and offensive language students know by sampling only their speech in class. You need to listen to them conversing outside of your classroom: in the hallways or during lunch periods.

Language Values Project

Most language research begins with a period of observation. An interesting project involves monitoring your students in a variety of different non-classroom settings. Start listening to and recording what your students are saying at extracurricular events and in the hallways and on playgrounds and sidewalks before, during, and after school.

Make a list of who says what to whom. How are boys insulting other boys? If so, what words are used? How are boys and girls insulting each other? Are there noticeable conflicts between different religious or ethnic groups in your school? What dirty words are used most frequently? Which dirty words and expressions seem most offensive and hurtful? Are your students bringing slang into your classroom from television and radio? If so, what words and phrases are they picking up?

Until you can answer these questions about the language that your students use, you cannot understand students' language values and how these values are established. Language is a powerful indicator of socialization and each student places different values on learning conventional speech versus street language. Some students are conformists while others run against the tide.

Popular Culture

One powerful influence on our children is popular culture, especially television and music. Children identify with fictional characters in their favorite television shows. Students memorize jokes and insults from popular offensive programs and repeat the inappropriate language at school. They identify with their favorite musical groups and repeat their favorite songs. They wear clothing and merchandise sponsoring their favorite figures in popular culture. Some of these popular influences are at odds with school and parental values, especially those advocating drug use, violence, discrimination, and promiscuity. Popular culture is explored in more detail in chapter 27.

Personal Identity

In their quest to develop a sense of personal identity, older children adopt language values that differentiate them from their parents and other adults. When teachers and adults are able to decode students' slang, the students create and adopt new slang terms. Language and vocabulary are very personal for children, and they pay a great deal of attention to developing a style of communication that sets them apart from adults around them.

Children also use offensive language to infuriate adults and test the limits of authority. Teachers who adopt language standards that are too strict will be tested. Some students feel the urge to test every rule that is devised by an adult, and language rules will be put to the test. Students are especially attentive to double standards (adults can do something but children are not allowed) and hypocrisy (setting universal rules and not following them oneself).

Human Sexuality

Students who are learning about human sexuality acquire and use words for body parts, body products, and sexual behaviors. Teachers should be prepared to deal with unconventional slang terms on the topic of human sexuality. Teachers should be prepared to substitute acceptable clinical terms when students use vulgar terms. You may find that some students are unable to discuss topics in class such as birth control, abortion, sexually transmitted diseases, homosexuality, or even romance because they do not know acceptable or clinical terms that are less embarrassing than street language terms for "sex."

Summary

You do not have to speak the language your students speak, but you do have to know what students are talking about in your classroom. If your students use jargon, slang, and vulgarity, you have to have a working knowledge of it, especially if you have a homeroom or supervise lunch periods. Your students' values are influenced by popular culture, personality, human sexuality, and the local variety of slang. Start listening to them if you are not familiar with the jargon. Part Four explores student language values.

CHAPTER 16

What Are My School's Language Values?

E very school has a set of rules or policies affecting language use at school. The first place to look for school values is the written policy on the subject. Many schools have handbooks for teachers and students outlining appropriate and inappropriate behaviors. These behaviors include spoken language, recorded music, graffiti, printed T-shirts, and writing on baseball caps. The policy can cover language at school as well as that on the bus and on school outings.

Every written policy is a clear indication of your school's language values. Your school should outline a clear policy regarding verbal sexual harassment, disorderly conduct or fighting words, racial or gender discrimination, and the use of offensive language that is subject to restrictions both on campus or off. These school language policies should be reviewed and discussed with students from time to time. Unfortunately, teachers and students do not always conform to written policies and guidelines when it comes to speaking to each other.

A second source of school values can be gleaned from counselors and administrators who have dealt with problems with speech over the years. These people can inform teachers about points of conflict and potential conflict about language use that have occurred in the school in the past. Some of this information may be recorded as the

Your school's language values exist in written policies which uphold federal and state laws. You should know all the school policies affecting language use.

result of formal hearings, peer mediation, reports, or informal counseling. Certainly, novice teachers should be informed about policies and conflicts before they enter the classroom. School language is also subject to community scrutiny.

Parents and community members also influence school language policy. Community members, PTO groups, and students' parents may complain about their own children's or other children's language at school, sporting events, extracurricular activities, or traveling to and from school. If members of the community do not like the language they hear students using, teachers will be among the first to hear about the community's complaints.

Parents' Values

Not every parent or teacher feels that cursing is bad or that the use of dirty words is a problem that must be eliminated. Some parents and teachers worry less about vulgar or obscene expressions than physical violence, teenage sexuality, and drug use. Some parents use dirty words freely and permit their children to use offensive language, too. Although a particular teacher may have liberal or conservative language values, he or she has to uphold the school's policies, including those that differ from his or her personal language values.

Community Pressure

School values and policies depend on community pressures and economic, religious, and social forces within the community. Whether a school allows the use of dirty words or not depends on what values are placed on conventional language use and community concern. School neighbors, religious leaders, community leaders, teachers, and parents should support the use of good communication skills and appropriate language use.

Some families may be very religious and not tolerate any type of profanity or blasphemy at home. Some parents restrict the kind of television, music, or videos their children are allowed to watch because of the potential use of profanity in these media. Parents, rather than teachers, should teach their own children about why their family values are different than those of the family next door and how different families can have different rules about language in their homes. All community values come to rest inside your classroom.

Summary

Your school's language values exist in written policies which uphold federal and state laws. You should know all the school policies affecting language use on campus and at extra-curricular events. Your school's language policies are also subject to community pressures. You should educate yourself about existing student in- and out-groups. You should be aware of the prominent ethnic, social, and economic pressures in the community where you teach. If you feel that your school's policies are inadequate to deal with language problems, bring up the topic of offensive language usage at the next teachers' meeting or at the PTO meeting.

If you cannot work with the existent language policies, change the policy. Common sense and conventional standards should prevail if students are to graduate and fit into mainstream America.

CHAPTER 17

What Are My Language Values?

In order to determine your language likes and dislikes, complete the two worksheets found at the end of this chapter. Finish your own work before discussing your feelings with fellow teachers.

Worksheet 1: Language Values, Part A

To complete the first list in Exercise 1, go back through Part One of this book and skim the opening chapters on the different categories of cursing. Rate each dirty word, assigning it a value from 1 (not offensive) to 9 (extremely offensive). Make a list of the words and phrases on Worksheet 1 that offend you most when used by other people. List the words and phrases with offensiveness ratings of six or higher.

Speaker Gender and Status

Completing this first list will put you in touch with your reactions and values at the individual word level and tell you if you discriminate based on gender or status. Most of us are sensitive to speaker gender and age or status.

Does a speaker's gender or status (age) make a difference to you? Are female speakers more offensive than male speakers when they use dirty language? What about your students? Do you consider the same offensive words used by your students to be more or less

It is important for you to realize how YOU feel about dirty words.

offensive than when they are used by fellow teachers or other adults? Look at the words you listed and indicate if gender or age makes a difference with each word.

Types of Cursing

Now rank the categories of offensive words. Is the use of one type of dirty word more offensive than others? Did you consider obscenity more offensive than profanity or blasphemy? Are religious words more offensive to you than sexual speech? Maybe you are the kind of person who finds all types of nonstandard language offensive. Maybe you have religious values that make profanities more offensive than obscenities. Perhaps you find gender-related insults or references to sexuality most offensive. Your ratings, use, and reactions to offensive language tell you who you are, and the ratings reflect your values.

Next, determine your language values by examining your reactions to film or television language or the different types of jokes you hear. Your preferences for certain types of movies, television shows, music lyrics, and humor should be related to the kinds of entertainment you enjoy.

Each person has a different sensibility or preference for motion pictures, music, and humor. Adults tend to be more stable in their preferences versus dislikes. Teenagers, on the other hand, are different and will experiment with different styles and identities. Students may prefer to admire anything that adults find disgusting. You should find that many of your close friends have similar values with regard to language and entertainment preferences. Your fellow teachers and administrators may have more diverse preferences than your closest friends. Modern schools are staffed by a diverse group of people with different values, especially schools in metropolitan areas.

Worksheet 1 tells you about your reactions to dirty language in both printed and spoken forms. But what about applying your reactions to spoken language problems in the school context? What happens when you are confronted with offensive language at school? What happens when you hear yourself using offensive language?

Before involving other faculty in a discussion about cursing, note what you say to others at school. Under what conditions do you curse? What offensive language do you hear from others around you? Keep a record of the speakers, times of day, and causes of the cursing in the table at the end of Worksheet 1.

Worksheet 2: Language Values, Part B

Worksheet 2 further examines your values and makes comparisons with fellow teachers. Judge which words on the list you find acceptable, inappropriate, or unacceptable for use at school. Acceptability judgment or rating is one method teachers can use to develop school language policies, the topic of the next part of this book.

You may want to compare your ratings and notes with the notes of other teachers who are interested in cursing to determine similarities and differences in language values. Worksheet 2 also prepares you for Part Four.

Who Owns the Language Problem?

Once you have a more accurate view of your language values, you can begin to appreciate the differences in values among you and other teachers and students on campus. It may be the case that you have a problem listening to people who use mildly offensive language. For example, teachers seem to be much more offended by the word "sucks" than children are. To children, "sucks" means "bad" and nothing more. If you are hypersensitive, you have to take some of the blame for a language problem.

It may be that your students have a problem using offensive language. They must take the blame and change their speech patterns. Problems can also be shared. Older teachers are somewhat intolerant of mildly offensive speech, and students are indifferent to it. In this case, both parties own the problem, and both must make adjustments toward using appropriate speech.

It is important for you to realize your language values. Your perception of cursing affects the way you enforce the rules you set for your classroom. You can manage best the rules you believe in the most. Many teachers attempt to enforce rules in which they do not believe. Many teachers use forms of discipline in which they do not believe. Students recognize situations when a teacher does not trust or support the rules because the resultant discipline appears to the students to be enforced inconsistently. Having an accurate perception of your own values and views on classroom discipline helps you manage more effectively. If you know your values, you can devise classroom rules that reflect these values, and you can enforce behavior management techniques that support your values.

Summary: Values, Standards, and Context

It is clear that standards change according to contextual variables. Most students readily accept and observe the rule that obscenities and cursing have no place in the classroom. Elsewhere, like walking home from school, students perceive that they have a right to express themselves as they want. In other words, different standards or values emerge depending on a student's surroundings. Similarly, multiple values arise for teachers. A few teachers feel that language rules are an invasion of free speech and think they have the right to curse in class. Other teachers adopt multiple standards for speech; the standard for the classroom is different than standards used in public or in private settings. Therefore, do not be puzzled by students and fellow teachers who shift speech patterns in different social-physical contexts. By completing the worksheet exercises, you will see your own values at work.

Worksheet 1: Language Values, Part A

List words from Part One with ratings from 6 to 9. These words offend you the most.

Considering how you rated the above words, rank the following categories from most offensive to least offensive to you: slang, profanity, blasphemy, scatology, harassment, vulgarity, racial slurs, insults, and obscenity. What does this rank tell you about your personal values?

List the words from papers, television, movies, and so forth that offend you most.

List cursing episodes you hear at school. Indicate the speaker, words, and cause.

Speaker / Target	Words Used	Cause

Worksheet 2: Language Values, Part B

Words and Values: Rate the offensiveness of each expression from 1 (not offensive) to 9 (extremely offensive). (Space is provided at the end for additional expressions.) Classify as profanity, slang, obscenity, harassment, racial slur, insult, scatology, or vulgarity (more than one type is possible). Indicate if it is inappropriate (I), acceptable (A), or unacceptable (U) at school. Do your students use it (yes [Y] or no [N])? When you are finished, compare your answers to those in the exercises in chapter 17.

Expression	Rating (1-9)	Semantic Classification	Acceptability (I, A, or U)	Use (Y or N)
prick				
fuck you				
asshole				
nice tits				
this sucks				
son of a bitch				
nigger				
dillweed				
dummy				
hell				
spaz				
teacher's pet				
shit				
bitch				
queer				
asswipe				
butt				
motherfucker				
shit for brains				
big mouth				

pussy				
spic				
christ				
toad				
cute ass				
asskisser				
fag				
whore (ho)				
jock				
fart				
fucking asshole				
creep				
dork				
on the rag				
cunt				

PART THREE

Setting
Standards

CHAPTER 18

Setting Priorities: Which Values Are Most Important?

The first priority in education is instruction. With that in mind, the most important language priorities are those that *have to* be met. The most important priorities must appear in a written document for members of the school community to read and discuss. If your school does not have a written policy, it should seriously consider such a document. In addition to major priorities, some secondary, local, and community issues may also appear in the written policy. However, most of the secondary language priorities are classroom rules and guidelines from teachers. The most important language guidelines to enforce are those mandated by federal, state, and local laws. Obviously, these guidelines cannot be ignored.

The second most important guidelines are those set by school policy and community standards, which vary from region to region. Faculty and students must be aware of their rights and responsibilities regarding appropriate language as mandated by law. New teachers must also pay particular attention to rules and requirements in their students' handbooks. After legal considerations have been addressed, teachers should set individual classroom priorities based on the three Rs: reason, respect, and responsibility.

Many common-sense language values can be based on reason, respect, and responsibility.

Federal and State Laws

Federal court rulings make it clear that language in schools must be restricted in several ways. We are not free to say whatever we please. Students and teachers cannot use language or comments that would constitute a form of sexual harassment; that has been made clear by recent court rulings. Students and teachers cannot use language that would constitute a form of racial, gender, or ethnic discrimination (or bias) as indicated by civil rights laws and Title IX of the Education Amendments. New teachers must be familiar with these laws.

Schools and teachers who permit illegal language could be sued in civil court for damages. Penalties for ignoring students who are being harassed or abused have been upheld in state courts. Schools have been forced to provide for compensatory monetary damages. Schools which do not uphold federal laws run the risk of losing federal funding.

At the state level, each state has a different set of criminal laws regarding disorderly conduct, fighting words, graffiti or vandalism, and hate crimes. State laws may be more specific than federal ones with regard to words and conduct that are restricted. Most noticeable are "fighting words" statutes, which depend on the cases that have been tried in each state. People who break state laws are subject to criminal prosecution as well as penalties proscribed by law.

Community Standards and School Policies

After teachers and administrators are certain they understand the importance of upholding federal and state laws and have incorporated them into school policy, the next set of priorities is to be derived from more local sources. Sometimes communities adopt more stringent or restrictive laws than are developed at federal or state levels. Conservative communities may have greater restrictions on teenagers' behavior such as imposing curfews, restricting skateboarding, loitering, and congregating and eliminating hangouts.

Some communities may restrict the use of offensive language in public and private locations such as museums, shopping malls, parks, and recreational areas. For example, some types of bumper stickers, T-shirts, or printed hats have been banned in different communities around the country. In one instance, people wearing offensive T-shirts were prohibited from entering a museum in Chicago.

Many schools have forbidden the wearing of shirts or caps that promote alcohol or drug use or ones that depict suggestive language or language which is offensive to members of the school. A "Coed Naked" T-shirt is one example. These guidelines affect students not only at school but also during field trips and the use of school facilities after school or when traveling to and from school.

States, or smaller communities within them, may have restrictions on the explicitness and nature of sex education materials. Restrictions may apply to sexual language or restrict graphic pictures of genitalia or sex acts. Some sex education materials may be subject to school board approval, parental consent, or other sanctions prior to their use in the classroom.

With legal issues covered, language policies and values can rely on language priorities which stem from common sense and good conduct. Common sense language values are based on reason, respect, and responsibility.

The Three Rs: Reason, Respect, and Responsibility

Children are not born with a knowledge of dirty words; they learn dirty words by interacting with other people early in life. Teachers should realize that it is normal for children to hear and use offensive language. Ultimately, each teacher must address the question of how to respond to students who curse at school. How can we teach students about the appropriate use of dirty words in the context of differing family and community values? First, we use wisdom and reason.

Reason

When a student uses a curse word, do not immediately blow a fuse and physically punish him or her. Ask why he or she said that. Act in the student's best interest. Assess the student's emotional state.

Why is the student angry, agitated, or surprised? School-aged children can be reasoned with, and you can explain the rules restricting the use of curse words at school. I describe different kinds of language rules in Part Five.

To act with reason is to have a purposeful and thoughtful basis for one's actions. To use reason means to approach the use of offensive language as a problem to be solved. Cursing episodes should neither be ignored nor blown out of proportion. Competent teachers demonstrate the ability to reason by thinking about what they are going to do about cursing before they act. Competent teachers are not impulsive, irrational, inconsistent, or abusive toward children. Competent teachers treat their students reasonably and respect students' rights.

Through the use of reason by teachers and students, we intend for students to internalize or memorize the rules for proper language usage. With the internalized rules of etiquette, students begin to exercise self-monitoring of communication and self-control. With reason and self-guidance, students gain a sense of respect for other people, the next topic for discussion.

Respect

Respect means consideration for others' dignity and regard for individuality. Many people verbally abuse each other because they do not respect others' rights to be different and to express differing views about religion, ethnicity, or sexuality. "Respect" refers to our use of personal space, control of one's body and physical movement, and the pursuit of happiness. Calling people names and using insults based on real or imagined individual differences is generally disrespectful and violates the victim's personal rights.

Respectful people do not treat individual differences as bad. Calling classmates names based on superficial characteristics such as physical appearance, food preferences, or gender differences fosters stereotypical and derogatory attitudes about those who are different from the speaker. Bigoted attitudes expressed in communication in the form of insults, slurs, or jokes are disrespectful. Disrespectful student comments must be suppressed and replaced with appropriate language.

Students, by learning appropriate communication strategies, can eliminate superficial and trivial differences as a reason to insult a fellow student. Respectful children are more tolerant of the individual differences around them.

Some teachers promote the use of the golden rule of "do unto others..." to teach about mutual respect. The golden rule applies for children old enough to understand it. It requires the ability to empathize and take the other's point of view. The golden rule method can be successfully used to stop a student from referring to girls as "bitches." Empathy and understanding foster respect. Although young children have difficulty taking others' points of view or experiencing empathy, middle school students are intelligent enough to understand another person's point of view and empathize with classmates.

For many of us, respect is a conditional response. Giving respect to another person depends on whether he or she has earned our respect. Earning respect requires time and trust. For many people, once respect is lost through misbehavior or mistrust, it can be difficult to regain. Teachers, and other authority figures, initially receive respect from students without question due to a teacher's status and occupation. Teachers build respect through reasonable interactions with children. Teachers can lose a child's respect through lack of reason, inattention, and failure to empathize with his or her problems.

Students count on adults to be smart, reasonable, and authoritative. Children earn their parents' respect by demonstrating that they can behave in a responsible manner. Students who do not cooperate with teachers and continue to break rules are bound to lose a teacher's or parent's respect.

Adults who make rules for students but do not follow the same rules, experience difficulty maintaining students' respect. In many cases, adults set bad examples for children. If a man calls his wife a "bitch" in front of their children, the children learn the meaning of the word "bitch" and that their father does not respect their mother. Children generally learn respect by watching their parents interacting. We cannot expect students to learn and demonstrate respect for others based on disrespectful adult examples. Adults who set abusive and disrespectful examples raise children who repeat the same type of disrespectful behavior when they become adults. Consider some of the following suggestions for building respect.

- *Teachers:* Teachers should respect a student's right to be angry and upset. Give older students time to deal with their problems on their own before intervening or discussing a student's problem. Students expect teachers to be fair and in control. When considering problem solving strategies for behavior problems, remember to respect a student's right to be different and to exhibit individuality and creativity and a student's needs for privacy and emotional expression.

- *Students*: Children must learn to respect a person's right to exist, be different, and express different opinions and emotions. Students should respect other students' property and bodies. Students should not intimidate each other by damaging or destroying each others' property. Students must not physically abuse each other by pushing, shoving, hitting, or yelling. Language restrictions make little sense if physical threats and intimidation are allowed to go unchecked at school.

Responsibility

Responsibility means that teachers and students are accountable for their behavior. One takes blame for one's mistakes. To demonstrate responsibility, a student has to have free will to make choices. Sometimes students make the right choices, and other times they make the wrong choices. When a problem persists and a student continues to make poor decisions, someone has to take the blame or responsibility for the behavior. Either the teacher or the student "owns" the problem in question. Sometimes teachers and students do not take responsibility for their problems. They make their personal problems other peoples' problems and blame others for mistakes. When a student curses in school, ask yourself who owns the problem. Who is responsible?

Assigning blame for cursing episodes is contextual and depends on the nature of provocation, mitigating circumstances, the student's level of self-control, and the coping strategies available to deal with stress. Responsibility means applying good judgment to make the right choices about rules, standards, moral behavior, and conventions. It means that a student has to take the blame or responsibility for breaking the teacher's classroom rules.

Once the teacher has expressed a language value in the form of a rule for the entire class, students have to use good judgment and conform to the rule. For example, if the teacher says, "Do not say hateful words in this room," the students now have the responsibility to obey the rule. A student who chooses to break the rule then owns a language problem and has failed to act responsibly. Good communication requires responsibility and responsiveness to others' needs.

Good communication skills develop when the speaker keeps the listener's needs in mind. When a speaker tailors speech to meet the needs of the listener, then the listener has been treated as an individual. Keeping the listener's needs in mind acknowledges a listener's individuality. Speakers and listeners have a shared responsibility to engage in effective communication.

It is the speaker's responsibility to develop good communication skills so that he or she can be precisely understood by listeners. Alternatively, listeners are responsible for being attentive and understanding. Communication is a shared responsibility between listeners and speakers. Speakers implicitly decide to take turns speaking and listening, and one must not attempt to dominate a conversation or talk too long. Speakers must try not to confuse listeners or waste listeners' time. Speakers must not openly use offensive, vulgar, or hurtful language without good reason.

Speakers should be aware that listeners form impressions of a speaker based on the language he or she uses. Hence, this is a good reason for a student to appear educated! A speaker is perceived and judged by the words and phrases chosen and how the words affect others. Once one starts speaking, judgments about a speaker's education, social status, stereotypes, and preferences are made.

Worksheet 3: Language Priorities

This discussion of priorities ends with a worksheet designed to help you establish language guidelines based on pertinent laws and general practices used by schools to govern students' behavior. First, we ask you to examine Worksheet 2 from Part Two, where you rated words for offensiveness and acceptability. We want to use that information to sort different types of language into Unacceptable, Inappropriate, and Acceptable categories. Unacceptable language is that which violates sexual harassment, discrimination, disorderly conduct, or vandalism laws. Unacceptable language includes obscenity, racial slurs, graffiti, gender-related insults, and any conduct outlined in school policy; T-shirts, gang signs and colors, jewelry, and language on buses are examples. There is no tolerance for unacceptable language, and the use of it is not sanctioned. Inappropriate language includes milder forms of profanity, blasphemy, slang, vulgarity, and scatology. Students are generally not punished for using these mild words but are told not to use them at school. Acceptable language is obviously good language, but acceptable language may also include some mild slang and vulgarity that are so widely used in colloquial English that they are acceptable but undesirable to educated adults. Words like "sucks," "crappy," "puke," "wimp," "chicken," "dork," "darn," "snot," "butt," "pig," "pee," or "barf" may be acceptable in some schools.

Summary

Implement language standards based on pertinent federal, state, and local laws. Then use common-sense values based on reason, respect, and responsibility to define good language. Finally, develop a three-level approach dividing offensive language into acceptable, unacceptable, and inappropriate categories.

Worksheet 3: Language Priorities

Give some examples of language that violates federal laws, state laws, or school policies. Refer to Worksheet 2.

a. sexual harassment (federal law)

b. discrimination (gender, racial; also consider federal law)

c. disorderly conduct or vandalism (state law)

d. specific school policies regarding language, conduct, or clothing (consult your school's student handbook)

List expressions of inappropriate language with low tolerance (students are asked not to use it but are not severely punished for mild infractions). List words from Worksheet 2.

List expressions of acceptable language which is tolerated (students may be asked to substitute these words in a writing assignment or exclude them from public speech). Check Worksheet 2.

Does your school's policy address all three levels of acceptability? Yes or No.

Are fellow teachers adequately informed about speech and law? Yes or No.

If you answered No to either question, you should talk to your administrators about a workshop or open discussion about language policies.

CHAPTER 19

What Does "Good" Language Sound Like?

For most Americans, good language sounds like what we hear from the television newscaster. Good language usually appears in newspaper columns and magazine editorials. I hope that the language in this book is considered an example of "good" language and that you could read passages to your students as examples. Good language is clear; it says what it means to say and is understood. Good language is concise and efficient; it uses only the words necessary to express the idea. Good language is precise; it uses the right words to express the exact idea that the speaker wants to convey to the listener or reader. Good language is grammatically correct and follows the rules of standard or conventional English. Good language is practical and effective; it communicates ideas to listeners or readers and has the right impact on them. Good communication is pragmatic; it allows speakers to take turns and share in conversations. It sticks to one topic at a time, and it efficiently uses, not wastes, a listener's time.

Given this description of what characterizes good language, mark which member of the following pairs of sentence uses good language. What rule(s) is(are) violated in the "bad" sentence?

Those who aspire to climb social ladders try to adopt a method of speaking similar to what they perceive as a prestige dialect.

1. It would probably be all right to turn in your papers at the end of the week.

2. Your papers are due on my desk by noon on Thursday.

3. I was feeling sorta shitty today.

4. I have a headache.

5. No, it's not finished.

6. Well, actually it's sort of like, you know, kind of not all done presently.

7. This sucks.

8. The homework assignment has more problems than I can finish in one night.

9. Personally, I, myself, am a family-oriented person.

10. I am family oriented.

11. If a person wants to succeed, they must get educated good.

12. If a person is to succeed, he or she must be well educated.

13. I am not going to put up with this kind of shit anymore.

14. Stop fighting or you will receive a suspension.

Some of the sentences violate principles of precision, grammar, clarity, and the efficient and effective use of a listener's time. Other deviations from good language are discussed below as we continue to describe language goodness.

The goodness of language for school children must be established between two language extremes. On the positive end, there is absolutely flawless diction, "correct" word choice, and syntax. On the negative end is sloppy, "uneducated" street language. Most educated speakers end up in the middle of the "language goodness" scale, not flawless but better than street language.

Newscasters are not flawless speakers, but they do produce a spoken language that obeys rules of propriety and broadcast standards, similar to the language standards that school children must learn for classroom discussions. Good printed language reads like that in a well-respected newspaper or magazine; students can read news items aloud to hear good language. These two examples of good language, written and spoken, are chosen to focus priorities on conventional language standards. Good, or conventional language, does not contain obscenity, indecent speech, or forms of offensive language listed in the first part of the book such as scatology, slang, ethnic or racial slurs, and vulgarity.

Spoken language, even from the best of speakers, is rarely flawless. Lectures and conversations from highly educated speakers are never perfect. Spoken language is filled with odd hesitations and filler words along with many grammatically incorrect constructions. The conventions for spoken language are always less rigid than those for print because writers have a lot of time to think about what they are writing as well as time to revise sentences. Spoken language can never be as precise as written language; "good" must be realistic.

Be Realistic: Develop Tolerance for Colloquial Speech

Language purists exclude the use of slang, vulgarity, and profanity from use under a strict definition of good language. Very few speakers in America have pure speech although the purists propose that speakers should try to be perfect. Realistic instructors believe that some colloquialisms are acceptable in classroom discussions. Some teachers think that slang and profanity have legitimate, although limited, uses in good speech. For example, slang or profanity might be acceptable in an essay to express surprise or anger or when used to describe dialogues within cultural subgroups like musicians or drug users. Students writing about street gangs would probably want to use some slang. These examples represent an effort to portray the language used in a realistic or authentic manner. Usually, slang is inappropriate but not unacceptable.

Colloquial language appears more frequently in literature, theater, film, and art than it ever has in the past. There must be some tolerance of colloquial language in the modern classroom. Each teacher must decide what is the proper place for slang, if any, within his or her classroom given the nature of the school, course of instruction, specific assignment, and community standards. Many teachers would have a difficult time teaching without using colloquialisms.

Prestige Dialects

Although perfect speech is an ideal, language communities do develop a particular model of communicating that is more highly regarded, or prestigious, than alternative local dialects. Within every speech community, those who aspire to climb social ladders try to adopt a method of speaking similar to what they perceive as a prestige dialect. Prestige dialects are those perceived as being used by the upper class and educated speakers in the community. The prestige dialect governs word choice, grammar, pronunciation, and intonation patterns. For our purposes, a "good" language does not necessarily have to mirror a prestige dialect in the local community to become a good form of classroom language.

Students from foreign countries, students with different ethnic or racial backgrounds, or students who were raised in different geographic regions (Boston versus Atlanta, for example) cannot be held to the same standards as those students heavily enculturated in white, middle-class America. Some tolerance of differences in dialect must be granted for the use of different accents, pronunciations, and word choices. Without linguistic tolerance, students with non-standard dialects and their language are stigmatized. Stigmatized students fail to engage fully in school work when they sense they are going to be ridiculed because of the way they speak. Good language is, of course, a relative term, and the definition must leave room for dialectal differences. Some guidelines follow for promoting good speech at school.

Guidelines for Promoting Good Speech in the Classroom

Rule 1: Teach Children Appropriate, Clinical Terms for Body Parts, Body Products, and Body Processes

If students learn clinical terms and only clinical terms, they then possess the appropriate language to express themselves about these functions. Additionally, you only have to teach students one set of words and not two. Teachers should avoid appearing anxious or angry with students when they have a need to talk about sex or take care of their bathroom activities.

Rule 2: Be a Good Role Model, Especially Under Periods of Stress

Adult speakers who use taboo words in anger or during periods of stress signal to the children, through emphasis on these words, that these powerful words are acceptable because an adult used taboo words. A student may later repeat these offensive words during a period of stress. Therefore, be a good role model and eliminate dirty words from your own expressions of anger.

Rule 3: Teach Students to Express Emotions Like Surprise or Anger without Using Dirty Words

Many students never learn how to express emotions appropriately at home. The burden of teaching guidance, self-control, and responsibility may fall on the teacher's shoulders.

Rule 4: Eliminate All References Considered Legally Obscene or Harassment or Language That Constitutes a Form of Racial or Gender Discrimination

The reason is simple, and the justification is straightforward. These references are illegal, and using these types of speech get speakers into a good deal of trouble with school officials.

Rule 5: Eliminate Racial Slurs, Insults, and Name Calling from Classroom Communications

These forms of dirty usage are disrespectful of others and treat others in a stereotypical fashion. These terms reduce individual differences across people to gross and superficial generalities.

Rule 6: Teachers Have the Right to Set Standards in the Classroom

It is your classroom. You are responsible for producing good speakers who will follow guidelines for good speech. The control of slang, vulgarity, and profanity within a speaker's written or oral communication is part of a good education. Do not make rules you cannot enforce or rules that you cannot consistently uphold.

Rule 7: Teach Children to Think About What They Are Going to Say, to Speak Slowly and Clearly, and to Listen to What They Are Saying

Most speakers make mistakes when they speak in a hurried fashion or when they are under pressure. Speakers also make mistakes while speaking with a lack of clarity about what they are thinking. Some students say, "I know what I want to say but I can't put it into words." These students are wrong! If you know what you are thinking, you *can* put it into words. If you cannot put it into words, you do not know what you are thinking. If you know it, you can say it. Monitor your thoughts and speech that expresses your thoughts (think, speak, and listen to yourself). If your speech does not make sense to you, it will not make sense to others.

Summary

Good language has identifiable characteristics and appears in newscasts and newspapers. Follow the rules and guidelines above. Be sensitive to dialect differences and the value of colloquial speech.

CHAPTER 20

What Student (and Teacher) Behaviors Violate Good Values?

Teachers and students have a shared responsibility to promote the of use good language in the classroom. Much of the effort to promote good language involves the suppression of offensive and substandard language while at the same time teaching and practicing conventional speech patterns and word choices. Students and teachers should strive to produce accurate and precise statements about what they are thinking and feeling. Many forms of substandard speech are vague and ambiguous, and substandard speech ultimately fails to meet the goal of being accurate and precise.

In all interactions among students and teachers, teachers and students must obey rules of conduct and laws. Although the laws are intended to be clear and not vague about issues of sexual harassment or discrimination, in reality many references and comments are ambiguous. It is not possible to determine if ambiguous comments would break the law without a thorough analysis of the context in which they occur.

Students may use offensive nicknames or words that are associated with a sexual act or physical appearance. On first hearing, nicknames and idiosyncratic terms may sound inoffensive. For example, students may refer to a girl with large breasts as " a cow," "big mamma," "jugs" or other words that are idiosyncratic or ambiguous in isolation. But maybe one of the boys has made a

A teacher who uses inappropriate speech or who allows students to use the same gives the impression that inappropriate speech is acceptable.

comment that her breasts were "large enough for a bird to perch on them." Then they begin to call her "perch." For those who did not hear the original reference in context, the word "perch" would not make any sense and certainly would not sound offensive at all. Unfortunately, in this instance, a young girl is being harassed with an idiosyncratic reference, and you are not aware of it because you do not know how the term was derived. If a teacher suspects that this kind of harassment might be happening but does not know what certain references mean, he or she might want to ask students a few questions about their terms.

What else can teachers do to maintain good language values? Teachers should attempt to rid classroom language of some popular teenage language customs such as repeating dirty words and jokes from television. In many cases, students are repeating these episodes to gain the attention of the teacher or fellow students. Paying attention to students who make these offensive interruptions only reinforces further use. Teachers should not call students names or use offensive language in class. Teachers should not belittle or insult students or use putdowns.

Teachers, as role models, must not use offensive language with students, and they should not allow students to use offensive language with each other. Insults, name calling, negative or offensive references to physical appearance or behavior, taunts, slurs, putdowns, and dirty jokes are not appropriate for classroom use. A teacher who uses inappropriate speech or who allows students to use the same gives the impression that inappropriate speech is acceptable.

Summary

Students are told that good language is required at school. They must eliminate name calling, harassing, dirty jokes, racial slurs, and other forms of speech that violate school policy. Students with substandard speech must be helped to gain appropriate language skills. Be a good role model.

CHAPTER 21

Setting Priorities

Which student behaviors should you change? Which should you accept? Which will not be tolerated? In order to set enforceable language standards, teachers and schools must have a set of priorities that indicate which language problems are most important and thus cannot be ignored. These important standards must be universally upheld and probably are associated with the most extreme penalties for violating them. These important language standards are those that are mandated by federal law. Our strategy for implementing priorities is to divide school language into three categories: unacceptable, inappropriate, and acceptable language.

Unacceptable language is forbidden regardless of context. These unacceptable words and comments are a top priority for elimination and suppression. Inappropriate language is that which is used in the wrong context; for example slang might be acceptable on the playground but not in classroom speaking and in writing exercises. Acceptable language is appropriate regardless of context and probably can be considered "good" language as discussed in chapter 19.

Students without good language never have the alternative to shift styles from formal to informal; they are stuck on the bottom rung of the language ladder.

First Priority: Eliminate Unacceptable Language

Forbid Language Which Results in Sexual Harassment

The federal courts forbid the use of language in schools that constitutes verbal sexual harassment. We printed the EEOC definition in Part One. Basically, the law forbids the use of comments of a sexual nature about a person's behavior or physical characteristics. The law forbids the telling of unwanted jokes of a sexual nature.

Forbid Classroom Language Which Results in Discrimination

Teachers must eliminate ethnic and racial slurs and words that demean people based on gender or religion in the classroom. This language would also include racist or sexist graffiti and printed words on clothing. These terms are unacceptable for teachers, administrators, and students. They are disrespectful and illegal.

Forbid the Use of Obscenity

Obscenity is not protected by First Amendment rights to free speech. It is very hard to justify the right to use it in a middle school setting. Restrictions on obscenity would appear in any written statements or written policies regarding students' conduct.

In these cases of unacceptable language usage, long-lasting, negative patterns of speaking and interacting in American society must be changed, starting with your students. Changing old habits is not an easy task, but a necessary task in order for students and teachers to feel safe and accepted in the classroom. Teachers and administrators must act with the best interest of their students in mind. Schools need to make a strong effort to overturn long-lasting negative language, thoughts, and emotions on campus.

Second Priority: Define Language That Will Be Tolerated but Discouraged

Strong Vulgarity

Vulgarity is the first class of language that is minimally acceptable in colloquial speech. Since we are in the business of educating students and making them sound educated, students who use vulgarity should be asked to find a different way to express the same idea.

Mild Scatology

Students come from a variety of home environments, and some of the their caregivers may not use clinical terms for body functions and body parts. Scatological references may be the only words some children know for these functions. Teachers should be tolerant of mild scatology from younger students and should encourage them to use more acceptable terms. Generally, as children grow older they begin to regard these words as childish and use more adult-like language, but some do not and need extra instruction, not punishment.

Third Priority: Teach Students the Tenets of Good Language

I describe the basic features of good language in chapter 19. Good language also implies the absence of bad language (which is controlled by teachers' reactions to it). Good language habits can be achieved when the teacher models appropriate language behavior in classroom exchanges and by helping students produce appropriate language when they are speaking in class. You can follow some of the guidelines in Part Five regarding the use of good role models for language. Our recommendations for promoting good language are simple: be a good role model, present good examples, and reward students' good speech.

Students learn that the classroom is a special context and that language used on the street is not acceptable there. A schoolroom is not the street corner; it is your classroom. Students must learn at this age that the mission of school is to develop students who can fit into mainstream American culture. Speaking appropriately is a worthwhile educational goal. Students who fail to acquire language skills will suffer in many areas of their life.

The rules and guidelines sanctioning students' behavior are established to benefit all students and to meet the goals of providing a good education. The rules are not made solely for the sake of control or teachers' peace of mind (although tranquillity may be one effect).

Fourth Priority: Define Language to Be Ignored

Although we encourage teachers to confront all obvious violations of school language rules, some mildly offensive language is encountered very frequently and is too mild to spend the time and effort to eradicate completely. We suggest teachers ignore some types of bad language. Profane euphemisms such as "gosh," "darnn," "holy smokes," or "jeezum" can be ignored. Mild vulgarities like "barf," "screw," "sucks," or "cruddy" are other examples. Very mild insults that have no effect on students such as "nerd," "silly," "introvert," "miser," "stick in the mud," "spoil sport," "crank," or "school girl" can most likely be ignored, but use your common sense and experience with insults. Inoffensive slang like "homies," "dude," "smokin'," "cool," "get real," "trolling," or "buzzed" can be ignored, assuming you know what it means. You may want to confer other teachers with this fourth level of priority and see what others are ignoring.

Summary

Teachers have to educate children, prepare them for life after school, and maintain order. In the end, students gain control of their own futures with the use of good language rather than being oppressed because they can only use inappropriate language or unacceptable speech. Students should come to realize that developing good speaking habits sharpens the mind. Students become better thinkers because they have to be better speakers. Once a student has learned good speech patterns, he or she can chose to use them or not, depending on the context. However, students without good language never have the alternative to shift styles from formal to informal; they are stuck on the bottom rung of the language ladder. Language priorities maintain order, uphold the laws, teach respect, and prepare students for life after school.

CHAPTER 22

Reality Check: What Does My Language Sound Like?

There are several reasons for teachers to check personal language use. First, teachers are role models, and we cannot expect children to improve their language skills if a teacher sets a bad example. Second, awareness of your own use of offensive language or your own use of substandard speech allows you to correct and improve your speech.

I recommend two methods of checking your own speech: a high-tech route and low-tech route. The high-tech route makes use of video or audio recording to document what is happening in your class. Either of the methods can be used covertly by hiding the recording equipment somewhere in your room. Note that you are not violating students' privacy if these tapes are used by you and you alone and are erased later (check with your principal or superintendent to be sure).

Using this unobtrusive recording method makes students in the classroom less apprehensive and produces a more accurate recording of everyday life in your class relative to obtrusive methods. A one-hour sample may be enough but you may want to record several different classes if the offensive language patterns differ among your classes.

If the unobtrusive measure is not appealing to you for whatever reason, then use an obtrusive method: tell the students that you are

You must determine if your language sample meets your own standards and those of the school.

making recordings of communication patterns in the class. You should probably make several hours of recordings in order to adjust for any "warmup" effects, caused by getting used to the equipment in the class.

The low-tech method can take two forms: the diary or the checklist. The diary system requires that you make entries on a frequent basis. These entries can be recorded as they happen: after each class or at the end of the day.

You should list any of your speech contents (words, sentences, or phrases) that seem substandard or inappropriate in any way. A checklist could be made by listing several types of speech errors that you anticipate on a sheet of paper and making several copies of the checklist.

When you make an error in your speech, you merely record the time of day and any relevant contextual information (who was listening, what you were talking about, or the significant emotions being expressed). While the checklist is faster than the diary, it may not contain as much information, and by using the checklist you are trading simplicity for detail.

Neither of these low tech solutions is as accurate as the high tech methods. You trade simplicity for details. There is no reason why a teacher cannot start with some audio recordings to examine the scope of his or her language problems and then switch to the simplified checklist system for a language update from time to time.

Either of these methods can be used with students in your classroom but why stop there? You may want to look at how you interact with other teachers on campus or at social gatherings. We suggest that several teachers get involved in speech monitoring and assemble for a social gathering and agree to record their own speech patterns for the purpose of improvement.

What to Look For

You can monitor your speech for several factors, depending on what you want to change in your speaking habits. You may look for improper grammar, types of offensive language, and interpersonal communication difficulties with teachers or with students (butting in, dominating, confusing, or not sticking to the topic).

Grammar

Check your speech for inappropriate grammar usage. Are you switching from your own dialect to a substandard dialect because of your students' speech? How do you respond to students' improper use of grammar? Do you correct them or let bad speech go? Some of these grammar standards may be related to your other language patterns. For example, you may permit both ungrammatical speech and the use of slang for some classes or students but not others.

Offensive Language

What kinds of offensive language are you using if any? You can use the outline in Part One to classify your speech (slang, profanity, and so forth). How do you respond when your students use offensive language? If you used an offensive term, how did your students react? One incident of cursing tends to lead to others.

Interpersonal Conflict

Do your language patterns change depending on your students' gender? What about race or intelligence? Do you speak differently in one class versus another? Do you use more slang in one class than another or permit the use of substandard grammar? Do you butt in, cut students off, change the topic, confuse students, or dominate a conversation?

Evaluation

Once you have collected some information about your own speech patterns, you can evaluate your language habits and compare them to others'. There is one problem that may be obvious to you: by monitoring your own speech and knowing that it is recorded, you are likely to change the way you talk. Generally, people change their behaviors when they know that they are being recorded. Sometimes just recording a negative behavior causes the behavior to occur less frequently. This happens with cursing, too. Merely paying attention to your thoughts and speech makes thoughts and sentences better.

Even though self-monitoring may be somewhat biased in the positive direction, it nonetheless provides objective information about how you talk at school. You should be able to name your most frequent problems and how many different problems you have to work on.

You can monitor your progress with the checklist, diary, or recordings over different time periods. You can give yourself a grade or compare your notes with another teacher or teachers interested in classroom language. Making these comparative judgments indicates whether or not you are similar to other teachers' standards, a judgment which may or may not be important to you. In the end, you must determine if your language sample meets your own standards and those of the school.

Summary

Do not tolerate unacceptable speech which violates the law or school policy. Change inappropriate speech that is too vulgar, offensive, or disrupts classroom decorum. Accept good speech and some forms of mild slang and mild vulgarity. Teach and model good speech habits.

PART FOUR

Why Students
Talk Dirty
and
What to Do about It

CHAPTER 23

Anger and Frustration

H ow can teachers help students to express strong emotions using appropriate language? There are many ways to express anger without cursing, but many students have not learned how to do that. Problems for teachers arise when students habitually curse when angry or frustrated. Other anger-related problems involve students who provoke or bully fellow students, causing victims to curse. Teachers have to deal with many kinds of anger and the situations which create anger. Teachers can deal more effectively with anger by trying to understand the emotion.

Anger is generally the result of frustration when one has been prevented from obtaining a desired goal. A person expects or wants one thing to happen, but something else occurred instead. He or she becomes frustrated, sometimes expressing negative feelings by cursing. Verbal anger expression is learned by watching others cope with frustration. In some cases, verbal anger is a more desirable expression of emotions compared to acts of physical violence.

Anger is a fact of life. It is part of the human condition. Cursing as a means of expressing anger is a habit to be broken. How and why children curse depends on how anger was learned at home. Many students come from homes where verbal aggression is a daily occurrence, and they assume that verbal aggression is an acceptable coping strategy for anger.

Young children learn to express anger by interacting with parents and others in the home. Parents and caregivers reward, tolerate, punish, and ignore emotional expressions. Each student has a

Try to understand why the child is angry in the first place and provide alternatives to cursing.

different learning history underlying his or her anger. Even though each child is different, there are stereotypes in our culture about how to express anger and frustration. One such stereotype is based on gender. Boys and girls learn different ways to express emotions.

What a student says when he or she is angry depends on what parents say when they are angry and whether parents punish or ignore a child's cursing. Each student's anger "training" comes to your classroom. Mothers and fathers may have different views about how to express anger, and they may discriminate between what sons can do and what daughters can do.

The gender issue has two dimensions, one at the student's level and the other at the adult's level. Fathers may be more physically punitive to sons than daughters. Fathers may allow a son to be physically aggressive, but they may allow a daughter to act like her brother. The mother may view anger as loss of control while the father sees anger as getting even. Daughters may learn to express their anger verbally while sons may be more physical when expressing anger. It all begins in the home.

Unlike parents, teachers cannot discriminate between boys' and girls' angry cursing. Teachers should train students to handle anger with the same coping strategies regardless of gender. Physical aggression is inappropriate for boys and girls; neither sex should be permitted to hit, pinch, push, scream, throw tantrums, or exhibit other types of physical coercion. These kinds of behavior are unacceptable and can be eliminated for both boys and girls with the same methods.

To cope with anger, teachers need to do two things: try to understand why the child is angry in the first place and then provide alternatives to cursing for a student when he or she feels angry.

Understanding Is the Key: As Simple as ABC

If a student gets angry at school and blurts out a "Goddamn it," you might be tempted to say "What did you say?" or "That was a stupid thing to say" or "Don't talk like that" or "I told you not to use that language." If you respond to an expletive used in anger with these reactions, you have made a big mistake. In each case, you have made the matter worse by challenging, insulting, confronting, or moralizing rather than understanding why the child was angry.

Consider anger from a motivational perspective. If your husband or wife suddenly shouted an epithet such as "Goddamn it" while you were shopping, what would you do? You would not react as you did with the student. You would ask your spouse what was wrong, or you would see if you could help your spouse in any way. The husband or wife response is the approach you should take with your students.

Dealing with anger is as simple as ABC: antecedent, behavior, and consequence. Try to understand why the student is angry. What is the antecedent? What caused the anger? Does is represent frustration? Was it provoked by another student? Was it accidental or premeditated?

Next, assess the meaning of the cursing behavior because the cursing reflects the degree of anger the student feels. What exactly was said? Was the cursing behavior justified? Is the student now cooling off or are emotions increasing? Was the cursing meant to harm or bully another student?

Finally, determine what the consequence or end result of the episode of cursing is. Should you punish the bully who instigated the cursing or the student who was bullied? Was the angry child responding to frustration or just trying to get some attention? The consequence of expressing honest frustration may warrant your sympathy and understanding rather than punishment.

Students who use aggressive behavior to victimize classmates deserve negative consequences (punishment). Bullying, insulting, hurting, and provoking other children cannot be tolerated. Students must learn that these types of anger-provoking incidents have negative consequences. The perpetrators must lose privileges or be punished rather than the victims who cursed because they were provoked. Bullies must also be taught how to deal with their emotions.

These are the ABC's. Teachers need to help frustrated (antecedent) children release their anger (behavior) without making their emotional state worse. Teachers should be sympathetic and understanding (consequence), not confrontational. When a child is angry, do not respond to him or her by being sarcastic, insulting, or insensitive, especially in front of classmates. Ask yourself, "What (antecedent) caused the anger?" "Are they cooling off (behavior), or are they losing control?" You need to be aware of the different forms of anger in your classroom. Help students express anger without using dirty words, but if they curse, deal with the anger first and then handle the cursing.

Not All Anger Is Equal: Epithets, Instrumental Anger, and Provoked Anger

When children get frustrated, they may have learned to vent the frustration through the use of a dirty word or an epithet which signals their feelings to listeners. Epithets are loud vocal outbursts of single dirty words such as "damn," "hell," or "fuck." Epithets may occur when a person is alone; for example, you hit your thumb with a hammer and say "damn." Frustration is enough to trigger an epithet. Another person does not need to instigate the use of an epithet. Epithets also occur in the presence of other listeners, but they primarily serve to express the emotions of the angry speaker.

Hearing an epithet informs listeners about the speaker's frustration and is thereby interpreted by the listeners as an indication of anger. The use of the expletive does not mean that the listeners are to blame; they are just innocent bystanders.

Anger may take two other forms that both involve the presence of other people as targets. These forms of anger are known as instrumental anger and provoked anger.

The distinctive feature of instrumental anger is that the speaker is using cursing to get a reward or reinforcement. The verbal aggression is an instrument used to obtain something. Instrumental aggression serves the speaker's needs. A speaker may swear at another in order to bully the victim into submission, to make others fearful, to exert power over the target, or to develop a reputation from peers as a student who knows how to curse well. In many instances, instrumental anger is premeditated or planned by the speaker to take advantage of a victim. In these instances, the cursing behavior is instrumental in bringing to the speaker some type of reward (power, status, attention, or reputation).

Instrumental anger serves the needs of the speaker through reward. Instrumental anger in the form of bullying and humiliating other students cannot be tolerated at school. Instrumental aggression must be eliminated through the loss of privileges, suspension, or punishment. Bullying and humiliating other students for one's own gain are inappropriate behavior for any school. The children must learn that bullying behavior has the consequence of punishment or loss.

Provoked anger is a reaction or response to an irritation. The distinctive feature of provoked cursing is that it is *a response* to a trigger rather than an instrument to get something from others. Provoked cursing is a reaction of a speaker to an irritating trigger. Generally, a fellow student triggers the speaker's cursing. The trigger could say something bad about the speaker, make fun of him or her, call him or her a name, or talk about some emotional issue that has caused an emotional reaction in the past.

Provoked cursing is an angry retort (behavior) to something someone said about you (antecedent). Provoked anger may be justifiable when speakers have been emotionally pushed into a corner. Psychologists speak of the "fight or flight" response when people in a stressful situation either flee the setting or fight with the instigator. Provoked anger is a fighting response.

Children frequently provoke each other, and in a sense provoked cursing is a justifiable response for a student who is being taunted. Common jargon refers to provoked anger as "pushing the right buttons" as if the reaction is a conditioned response to the provocation. Teachers should admonish the trigger person firsthand then teach the victim to express anger without cursing. When you realize that a student was provoked into cursing, you realize that he or she was not entirely responsible for the cursing.

Anger and Awareness

Some anger expressions are so habitually or automatically used that speakers curse without awareness of the cursing. It is common for people to lose their temper or become so frustrated and angry that they spill out a string of well-practiced words and phrases. The emotional level may be so high that the speaker pays no attention to what is being said, and the cursing language just comes out automatically. Later, due to the lack of awareness of cursing, the speaker has little or no memory of the exact words used in anger.

Whether the anger is instrumental, provoked, or automatic, a teacher needs to make a quick determination of why the student is expressing anger in a given context. Not all forms of anger are equal, and students have to be treated according to conditions that caused the anger. We do not want angry students to fight with triggers or ignore their strong emotions. We want to teach students to cope with anger-provoking situations without cursing by teaching them to use a variety of alternative strategies.

Teacher Strategies to Provide Alternative Methods of Expressing Anger

The first job for a teacher is to determine why a student is angry. Next, focus on helping the student begin to break old and ineffective habits such as cursing. Besides breaking old cursing habits, teach students new and alternative methods of expressing anger without cursing. When your students need to express anger, help them vent the emotion with some of the methods presented below.

Students must learn that cursing has its consequences. Students have to pay a price for cursing, and they must take responsibility for their own behavior. They should substitute acceptable, alternative forms of anger expression rather than cursing.

Counting to Ten

This method is simple. You ask the students to start counting softly from one to ten before they consider doing anything else. This teaches self-control and restraint. Counting to ten gives students time to think about what they are doing and allows their emotions to settle down.

Anger: Put It in Your Hands

Cover the mouth with both hands and let the emotion quietly flow out as if talking to yourself. Keeping the anger in the hands allows the student to express the anger in a more private manner and keeps them from disturbing other classmates. The students speaks into his or her hands about what is bothering him or her without yelling at another person. This is especially useful in an outdoor setting, recess, or play periods. The hands over the mouth become a signal to stop the flow of angry words at others. Eventually, holding back the dirty words will be achieved without putting the hands over the mouth. Younger children, through self-control, talk under their breath, quietly to themselves, rather than yelling out and escalating the situation.

Walking Off the Steam

If students get angry during recess, play periods, or during athletic competition, simply ask them to take a walk or a jog away from the group until they feel better. Walking or running helps dissipate the arousal in a positive rather than negative or aggressive manner. Walking off the steam prevents confrontation with other students, and it prevents escalation of the speaker's emotions.

Just Say, "I Am Angry."

Here is a good substitute for habitual dirty word users and will always work in expressing and reducing most anger. This allows the student to inform others about his or her feelings and the causes of the feelings.

Thinking Aloud: Informing and Describing

Here the angry victim informs the instigator about his or her anger. The victim describes what was felt during the anger-evoking event such as "When you stepped on my foot, it really hurt." This informing can be done without challenging, arguing, or yelling. It helps children negotiate their own problems with others without aggression.

What if no one provoked the anger? If he or she feels angry and another person is not responsible or another person is not involved, the thinking aloud routine allows the child time to develop self instructions to control and express the anger without doing something inappropriate. Later these vocalizations or self-talk can become a form of private speech and guide the student's behavior without cursing out loud.

Playing "Turtle"

Here the younger students are taught to close their eyes, put their heads down on a table or desk, clench their fists tightly, and think about what is the right thing to do or say. The turtle method prevents immediate expression of anger and replaces aggression with a quiet, incompatible behavior to deal with anger. It gives the child time to figure out what the right behavior is. Turtle works well with younger, less physical or aggressive children, especially in the classroom setting.

Summary

Understand the context of anger: what caused it, how it was expressed, and the consequences of being angry. Every student experiences anger. Cursing out in anger can be provoked when bullies victimize classmates. Cursing can also be instrumental in obtaining rewards for some speakers. Sometimes epithets are used to express frustration, and students may not be aware they are using bad language. Deal with emotions first and speech second. Teach students alternative methods of expressing anger and frustration.

CHAPTER 24

Poor Self-Concept and Low Self-Esteem

Children who have been accepted by their parents, teachers, and peers develop a positive sense of self-worth and feel secure. They generally interact with people using positive social behavior. Students who have experienced rejection at home and at school do not have good self-concepts. Rejected children feel insecure and threatened, and they have identity and personality problems. Rejected children become anti-social and withdrawn and may use cursing and foul language to distance themselves from others.

Dealing with the "Lows"

Students with long-standing low self-concepts (here referred to as the "lows") are difficult to change. Teachers, parents, and peers can help students develop better self-concepts by communicating to them positive expectations and responding to them in a positive manner. Low self-concepts can be elevated when children see themselves successfully completing challenging classroom assignments or coping with and solving their own problems. Students with low self-concepts need positive feedback, positive expectations for good behavior, and positive thoughts. Low self-concept and low self-esteem children need to experience success on a wide variety of academic and

Teachers can help students with personality problems by eliminating the negative statements that other students make in reference to them.

interpersonal tasks. When the lows fail at academic tasks, they may respond with anger and confrontations with other students, eliciting cursing and aggression. The lows need to be realistic about their potential and need to develop positive expectations about their future performance. Success for the lows, even on small tasks, helps to eliminate frustration, and it increases the lows' sense of self-efficacy.

Teacher Strategies for Low Self-Esteem Students

Focus on the student's existing academic strengths in the beginning. Build successful interactions from these strengths. If one's strength is reading or library skills, start working with these. A student's weak communication skills, achievement motivation, or task-completion can be repaired later.

Work on strengthening one skill at a time. It is difficult to change a student's overall perception of self-worth all at once. After library skills have been tapped, start working with task-completion.

Create a non-competitive, game-like atmosphere to decrease the stress of individual performance. Lower stress will produce less frustration and bad language. Try to eliminate the stifling atmosphere caused by competition.

Use group exercises when possible. Create an atmosphere of play and enjoyment from time to time, so that all students get a break from competing with each other. Monitor the lows, making sure they partake in the fun, too.

Learned Helplessness

A good deal of psychological research indicates that many children and older adults have deduced through repeated attempts that no matter what they do they will never be successful. Once a person adopts this attitude, the motivation to achieve is lost, even for very simple tasks. This attitude and resultant behavior is called "learned helplessness." In many cases, the lows' lack of initiative and cursing out of frustration stems from learned helplessness.

Teacher Strategies to Break the Cycle of Helplessness

Work with students one-on-one. Break the cycle with some minor successes. Get them engaged in some meaningful task. See that the task is completed as designed. Make sure helpless students see their successes. Verbally reinforce them for success. Change the students' perceptions and attitudes about helplessness by showing students that their previous perceptions about helplessness were inaccurate and that their negative attitudes can be changed.

Anti-Social Students

Anti-social students, as the adjective "anti-social" suggests, fail to conform to conventional standards. They fight with authority figures such as teachers, and they dislike "normal" students. Some anti-social students have a low tolerance for rejection along with a low frustration level.

Anti-social students need to be brought into the fold slowly, and challenges to their abilities and achievements should be increased slowly. Increases in their self-esteem are achieved through realistic challenges in the classroom. Dramatic challenges to anti-social students to make changes in their personalities will seem overwhelming to them. Students with low self-concepts will disengage from academic tasks that make them feel too anxious and fearful. They will regress to less mature levels of behavior (cursing and acting out).

Teacher Strategies for Anti-Social Students

Do not lose touch with anti-social students. Keep an eye on them, and do not let them fade into the back row of the class. Call on them in class. Ask reasonable questions (not too easy) and give adequate time for a response (several seconds).

Assign tasks and projects that require group interaction and individual responsibility. These activities require input from each participant, and the group can only be successful when each student participates.

Inform an anti-social student that you are willing to discuss a problem when he or she is ready. If peer mediators or tutors would be helpful, suggest that he or she might consider working with another student. If problems are severe, suggest that the student talk with a private counselor or the school counselor.

General Strategies for Difficult Students

Eliminate Name Calling, Insults, Putdowns, and Self-Directed Insults

The first order of business is to reduce the negative comments students make about each other. That is no easy task. You need to keep lows from putting themselves down in class. If you allow low self-concept students to denigrate themselves, they are perpetuating a type of self-fulfilling prophecy. The lows think they are bad, keeping their level of expectation and motivation at a very low level. This thinking that one is "bad" is used later to irrationally justify previous poor performance. The attitude-behavior-denigration cycle keeps spinning around.

Interpersonal insults among students and self-references to being stupid, slow, dumb, weird, lazy, or incompetent are very subtle but lie at the core of students' rejections. These putdowns are not social insults about being or not being in a group of people or belonging to some social-ethnic group. These insulting and denigrating descriptions about mental abilities are targeted at a student's poor performance in class.

After eliminating or reducing negative and rejecting statements, a teacher can begin a program to build self-respect and provide praise for all students. In this program, teachers target all students, including those students who have been rejected or neglected in your classes. Concentrate on those students who need the most help; do not let the lows slip out of awareness, something they seek to do.

Both High and Low Achievers Need Attention

But while the capable students seem to get enough praise on their own merit, the lows need special attention, so make sure they get it. Do not forget the lows or be put off by the antisocial students. Neglecting troubled students reinforces their perceptions and negative attitudes which affects their performance in class and interactions with other students.

Stimulate Students' Self-Reinforcement and Praise for Fellow Students

Low self-concept students need to praise themselves for their accomplishments. They also need mutual respect from peers. Other classmates, through mutual respect, can use praise with each other for progress on academic tasks. The use of praise is simple and uses language such as "I like the way you did your...," "Look what a good job Jeff did on his project," or "This work shows a lot of effort and improvement." You certainly can think of more.

Lows and antisocial students need praise but not too much praise because that would make these students too self-conscious and perhaps make them feel embarrassed. Such false rewards undermine genuine praise and decrease student motivation.

Develop Students' Self-Awareness and Their Ability to Set Realistic Goals

Help the lows realize their strengths and weaknesses. Make sure that they set goals for performance that are in-line with their abilities. Break the cycle of learned helplessness by getting students working and succeeding on meaningful tasks of their own choosing. Insignificant goals are not worth achieving, and goals that are out of reach are easily ignored.

Provide Choices to Complete School Assignments and Help Students Deal with the Consequences of Their Choices

Minimize competition among students and lessen the possibilities for failure and rejection. Increase cooperation among students. Create projects that require inclusion or participation of all students.

Help Children Cope with the Pressures of Growing Up on a Variety of Levels

Low self-esteem may be correlated with other social, academic and physical changes and challenges that students face. Failure in one area may breed failure in another area. Success in one area of life raises esteem and expectations in other areas. For example, students who become successful at sports may also raise their expectations for social interactions and classroom performance.

Self-esteem and personality problems are difficult to solve in a group situation, and individual students may need individual attention. However, teachers can help students with personality problems by eliminating the negative statements that other students make in reference to them.

Summary

Students experiencing low self-esteem, learned helplessness, and personality problems frequently use bad language. They are the targets of both self-directed putdowns and name calling from classmates. Eliminate negative statements and name calling. Pay attention to the lows and slowly try to get them involved with academic goals. Some students with severe problems may be beyond your help.

CHAPTER 25

The Need to Belong: In-Groups and Out-Groups

Belonging to a group is a fact of life for every normal student in school today. Students join athletic teams, music groups, academic clubs, and other official groups at school. Students also identify with and belong to the social groups unrelated to school such as those interested in religion, the 4-H club, stamp collecting, Star Trek, playing chess, the Boy and Girl Scouts, amateur sports, and other community groups. Belonging to a group is beneficial for children because group membership helps build a sense of sharing, responsibility, understanding, sensitivity to individual differences, and social cohesion in order to obtain group goals.

Cliques

One simple way to look at students' needs to belong to groups is through the cliques students form. Cliques are common in every school. As the old saying goes, "Birds of a feather flock together." Groups of students tend to assemble on the basis of common interests, backgrounds, or talents: athletes, rich students, poor students, smart students, vocational students, drug users, music and band members, antisocial and hostile students, party goers, sexually

Teachers and staff need to be aware of the personal and group-related pressures that affect students.

promiscuous students, drama students, neighborhood members, and gang members.

Each group has its own set of rules and expectations for members, including conforming to the group's conventions, habits, slang, clothing styles, jargon, attitudes, and beliefs. Group participation fosters positive social behavior as well as negative or antisocial behavior like cursing at other students and defying authority figures.

On a negative level, some students belong to groups which are bent on suppressing, denigrating, and showing aggression against other groups of students and non-students. A street gang is probably the most obvious example, but negative grouping does not end here. Students discriminate against each other based on skin color, body weight, educational ability, food preferences, parents' occupations, family income, neighborhood, ethnic status, dialect differences, and just about any other dimension of American life than can be used to differentiate the "have's" from the "have nots." Consider how groups affect students.

Teacher Strategy: Understand How Groups Think

Belonging Is Serious Business

Group conflicts involving gang violence, racial discrimination, gender discrimination, or sexual harassment cannot be tolerated at any level in school. Teachers must be aware of the social divisions that exist within the school district and be attentive to the earliest signs of intergroup rivalry. Any language or threats that could result in civil or criminal action cannot be used at school. Schools must have zero tolerance for criminal or civil infractions; abusive language is just one part of the problem.

Ethnic groups, street gangs, and social groups in schools develop distinctive styles of dressing and unique styles of speech. Students who want to identify with these groups, even if they are not members, emulate their role models. These differences in style and taste in dress, music, and language are the basis for insults and name calling among groups. Teachers who understand the distinctive features of one group versus another (long hair versus short, jeans versus slacks, and the color red versus blue) are able to identify putdowns when they occur.

Intergroup Rivalry

Competition is an inherent part of American culture, and competitiveness certainly is ingrained in students through our policies covering grading systems and ability-based standards for those who intend to enter college and professional schools. Competition is healthy to the degree that it promotes advances in academic performance for many.

Competition is unhealthy when it results in the use of putdowns, name calling, and insulting among competing groups of students. Students compete with each other for attention and status. Sometimes rising to the top means stepping on others. Even though the school may have a policy that forbids certain types of violence and cursing, students curse other students because they get more rewards (attention or status) from their reference group than punishment from the school. Teachers and staff members need to be aware of the personal and group-related pressures that affect students.

Gender, Diversity, and Maturation

The journey through puberty is a difficult one for many students. Pressures and messages from the media encourage children to act like adults, such as consume and spend, before they are intellectually, financially, or morally prepared to do so. Emerging secondary sexual characteristics (facial hair for boys and breasts and the beginning of menstruation for girls) are sources of conflict for students because sexual development produces obvious changes and differences in appearance. Any physical changes or differences among students can be sources of conflict and insults.

Late Maturation

Late development of secondary sex characteristics tend to be more traumatic for boys than girls. Boys who remain childlike while their peers start to mature become the targets of name calling and ridicule.

Early Maturation

While late maturation affects boys more than girls, the opposite is true for early maturing girls. The appearance of breasts catches the attention of boys and girls and may be the source of unnecessary comments about sexuality and appearance. If these comments are not eliminated early on, they can be the source of later harassment and discriminating speech.

Teach Students to Respect Diversity and Individuality

Students need to treat each other with respect, the golden rule. The bottom line on eliminating derisive language and debilitating intergroup rivalry is to foster tolerance for divergent styles and opinions. The problem for students is that most teens are scared to death to be perceived as weird or different, and they are more likely to conform to group consensus rather than develop a strong sense of individuality. However, students must confront and question the existence of stereotypical and narrow-minded thinking that develops in groups. Narrow-mindedness is a basis for discrimination and insults.

Dialect Differences

Teachers should be cognizant of the different dialects that are used within the community. Be careful to not stigmatize or put down students who do not speak a standard dialect. Do not allow other students to make fun of the way others talk in terms of dialects, accents, and foreign languages.

Individuality

Teachers should help students foster individual identity formation, uniqueness, and creative expression. Help students think for themselves. Ask students to express personal opinions rather than opinions that ameliorate group leaders. Help students evaluate their own limitations and strengths independently of what a group thinks about them.

Children and Family Differences

Unfortunately, for students with weak family structures or those in abusive homes, gangs and social groups may be used to replace the security that is missing at home. Children need guidance and support; they seek nurturing wherever and whenever they find it. If parents fail to provide a sense of guidance, safety, and support, then children turn elsewhere. In this respect, the values of the gang (or the group) become a more important source of identification than either home or school values because the gang is the source of support, nurture, and values for the children who join them. Like it or not, these gangs and groups serve a function or purpose for the members who join them, or these groups would not exist.

General Strategies for Dealing with Groups

Try to prevent intergroup conflict and rivalry in lower grades. Use cooperative activities and reconfigure a group's membership in class activities. Do not be punitive; instead instruct children about openness and acceptance at the earliest age. Use an episode of conflict to instruct the entire class.

Become knowledgeable about student groups and conflicts that exist in your school and community. Know the insults the groups use for each other. Do not tolerate intergroup insulting and name calling but instead respond to it.

Increase positive, cooperative activities and communication among all students. Stress the need for individuality as well as tolerance for diversity. Do not tolerate verbal attacks on students based on gender, ethnic, or social differences. When verbal attacks occur, respond by educating the entire class about tolerance.

Summary

Identifying and belonging to groups is natural for children. Negative effects occur when groups of students denigrate, suppress, or attack rival groups. Maturation, diversity, and ethnicity may be the source of language differences, inter-group rivalry, and conflict. Teach students to respect differences and to think for themselves. Eliminate ethnic and racial slurs.

CHAPTER 26

Inappropriate Adult Role Models

Teachers should have a program which identifies good role models. Teachers should draw attention to and praise students who emulate good role models in oral or written assignments. A positive approach to good speech may dampen the effect of negative role models and substandard speech on young students. Unfortunately, problems with offensive language do not end by drawing attention to and praising good role models.

Students searching for their own identities sometimes emulate the vulgar speech and antisocial behavior of improper adult models. Negative adult models are found in some homes, the community at large, and in popular culture. Students pay a great deal of attention to movie stars, television actors, and popular musicians, who are sometimes the worst abusers of good speech.

Depending on the relationship between a student and an adult role model, the ties between them can be very difficult and sometimes impossible to break. Children who come from abusive homes or homes with adults who are chronic substance abusers are difficult to reach and change. Some students grow up without a proper adult model, and they never learn how communicate properly or how to treat others with respect and understanding.

Children generally learn about respect by watching how their parents treat each other. A student who grows up in a home with a heavy dose of disparagement has little opportunity to learn about proper respect. Parents, especially the same-sex parent, are usually the most important element in the development of a child's personal

Students who start to imitate and identify with the undesirable characteristics of adults should be re-educated.

identity. Students who chronically watch one parent being victimized or abused by the other may develop the negative traits of the same-sex parent. Teachers frequently witness students' identity problems in the classroom. And for a victimized student, later in life the abnormal patterns of communication and abuse learned in the home may reappear in his or her intimate relationships.

In many cases, teachers provide the weakest link to a student's emerging identity. Therefore, as a teacher you must always act in the best interest of the student and set a good example yourself—do not curse in front of your students or *you* become a poor role model. Demonstrate to students how an adult treats others through respect, reason, and responsibility. What are other factors related to students' witnessing poor role models? These other factors are covered below.

Confront Improper Adult Attitudes

Aside from adults who have questionable habits and lifestyles, a more insidious problem arises from adults' expression of prejudiced, stereotypical, or bigoted attitudes. Adults, especially parents, transmit to children negative attitudes about women, politics, welfare, income, education, minorities, religion, homosexuality, and other aspects of modern life. Many of these negative attitudes are the product of intolerance, ignorance, and narrow-minded thinking. Teachers experience negative student attitudes among middle school students who are asked to speak out on social-economic issues. Be prepared to respond.

Respond to and Inform Students about Negative Role Models

Some students use ethnic slurs, gender-related putdowns, and other insults at school because they learned them at home or in the street. Students who start to imitate and identify with the undesirable characteristics of adults should be re-educated. Students should be told that some adults' speech is improper.

First, children must be informed that the behavior or language in question is improper for use at school. An explanation, as to why the speech is improper (it is wrong, disrespectful, or prejudiced) can also be offered if necessary. Finally, an alternative or alternatives for expression in an appropriate manner should be offered. Using this method, improper role models are identified, their behavior is put into question, and alternatives are suggested.

Students should be urged to think for themselves and use good sense to determine whether an adult is a good or bad role model. Students should consider whether identification with a person will get them into trouble or lead to a difficult, troublesome lifestyle. Many students, developing their own identities, question adult authority figures. Getting students to focus on bad role models takes advantage of that natural tendency to ask questions.

Again, identity is a difficult psychological variable to change for some students, especially those who have been rejected, those who are alienated or who have low-self esteem. Students have to be convinced that a change in their lifestyle is in their best interest before they begin to consider changing.

Show Examples of Good Role Models in Your Classroom

One alternative to dealing with negative role models is to institute a good role model program for your classroom. Each week a different student with consultation from the teacher could select or nominate a popular figure to be the class' role model of the week.

Here you can play a critical role in defining what a good language role model is for teenagers. Eliminate superficial, rich and famous people in media and search for men and women of substance who speak well. Consider the speech of James Earl Jones, Sidney Poitier, Mario Cuomo, Connie Chung, Martin Luther King, Hillary Clinton, or Janet Reno.

It would be important to focus on the language that a good role model uses and perhaps present a video or recording of the person speaking in public to reinforce and emphasize the use of good language and speaking skills to your class. Maybe one of the criteria for selection to the weekly honor would be good speaking skills.

Use the News to Show Why One Should Not Use Inappropriate Language

Every week the newspapers and networks report on famous people who get into trouble for what they have said. Jimmy the

Greek, Marge Schott, Jesse Helms, Ronald Reagan, Dick Armey, and plenty of others can be the source of examples of what happens when we do not use appropriate language.

General Strategies

Do not passively accept the attitudes and language that students bring to school from bad role models. Challenge the ideas and speech of poor role models and replace the bad with good. Show how the use of inappropriate language can hurt a speaker. Be a good role model yourself. Provide examples of the speech of good role models or institute a good role model program. Draw attention to and praise your students' use of good speech.

Summary

Inappropriate language models can come from home, on the street, or in media. Confront and change improper attitudes. Indicate the consequences of bad speech. Identify good role models and reinforce good speech in class.

CHAPTER 27

Popular Culture

Popular culture in the form of television, radio, music, clothing styles, magazines, and movies exert a tremendous influence on the behavior and language of children. In some cases, these media set the standards for dress and language that are deemed more important than other adult standards and values. Teachers need to understand how popular culture influences student communication.

Educate Yourself

Be knowledgeable about aspects of popular culture that influence your students. When you cut yourself off from the television and music that students are consuming, you eliminate a possible channel of communication. When you limit the communication with your students, you become increasingly different and remote from students, and as a result you fail to understand each others' values.

You do not have to enjoy the popular culture, but you do have to have an informed and knowledgeable opinion of it. Simply put, understanding your students' values within popular culture is necessary to establish common ground for discussions and keep in touch with your students. Students appreciate your points of view about their language and culture.

You do not have to enjoy the popular culture, but you do have to have an informed and knowledgeable opinion of it.

Use Popular Culture to Your Advantage: Find a Teachable Moment

Ask your students what they like. If you are "up" on popular figures and fads, ask your students what their favorite movies, movie stars, television shows, music, music groups, and heroes are. If you get responses that are unfamiliar, do some research or ask your students about these people.

If you are knowledgeable about the movies and television shows that your students are watching, you can refer to the shows as examples of language usage in class discussions. If you know popular superstars, athletes, and heroes, you can use them in class as examples of good and bad choices in lifestyles.

Using Language on Television

Television is probably the most powerful socializing force in the culture (besides parents). Your students consume four to five hours of it a day. Popular shows are the source of jokes, jargon, and style for children. Each year new shows appear and old ones are canceled; unfortunately, they tend to become more offensive each season. One result of students' television viewing is that teachers find their students talking about the previous night's popular shows on a daily basis.

Use television shows (and other media) for teachable moments. Take an example from a show and indicate how bad language or behavior got the star into trouble. Some of these shows are filled with vulgarity and slang and may be held up as bad examples of proper speech for your class. Many of the characters on these shows who use offensive and inappropriate speech are far from model citizens, and they lead less than desirable lifestyles.

Comment on Examples of Bad Language in Music and on MTV

Since the inception of the teenager in the 1950s, our culture has created a genre of music guaranteed to turn off adults. Besides, if students' parents and teachers liked the same music as students did, the students would listen to something else.

Teenage music is designed to accentuate the differences between children and adults. If you check the "people in the news" section of the paper, you frequently see figures from the music industry getting into trouble for what they have said or done.

One area in the music industry that has been a source of trouble for school children is the genre of rap music, especially gangsta' rap which has drugs, guns, sex, and violence as its main themes. Loose women, police, adults, and authority figures are ridiculed and disrespected or "diss'ed."

MTV has been criticized for promoting violence, sexism, and commercialism in the popular videos. Teachers who view controversial videos like Madonna's have plenty of material for discussions with students.

Discuss the Positive and Negative Aspects of Motion Pictures

Motion pictures are less insidious than television and generally less offensive than gangsta' rap music. Teachers readily admit that movies and movie stars influence on children's behavior at school. If you pay attention to the figures that children regard as heroes, a great deal of them come from movies and television. Therefore, teachers need to keep up with students' movie interests to see what affects classroom speech from these films.

Again, examples of both good and bad behavior can be grounded in movie scripts. When you bring examples from popular films into class discussions, you have immediate common ground with many students.

Summary

Inform yourself about popular media. Try to understand why your students are attracted to negative aspects of popular culture, especially those from television, film and music. Use popular culture to educate students about language. Realize that today's fad will be tomorrow's old news.

CHAPTER 28

Negative Attention Seeking

Negative attention seeking occurs when a student does something undesirable in order to get the teacher's and/or other students' attention. Generally, the attention, even when it comes in the form of negative comments, punishment, or threatened punishments, is rewarding to the disruptive, attention-seeking student. Attention-seeking behavior patterns through the use of negative behavior may have been established at home before the child headed off to school. Children get a good deal of attention from parents when they act up.

Students Use Bad Language for Shock Value

Students will use cursing to get your attention. When a student curses, do not act shocked, upset, provoked, moralistic, confrontational, or angry. If you respond in this manner, you are giving the disruptive student the reward he or she desires, and the disruptive language increases in frequency. The more attention you give to cursing, the more likely that the cursing will persist. The secret is to not pay attention to mild disruptions or first-time occurrences.

Strategy: Simple Extinction Works

One way to deal with disruptive behavior is to ignore it and thereby extinguish it. Deal with a disruption in a calm and rational manner.

Do not get shocked, upset, provoked, moralistic, confrontational, or angry.

You have to be very consistent here to get extinction to work. Once you decide to ignore a student's attention-getting ploy, you must force yourself to never pay attention to the negative behavior again; otherwise, you run the risk to teaching the student that he or she has to use it many different times before it works on you.

If the student is getting attention from other students, the disruptive behavior may increase in frequency because it is being reinforced. You would have to eliminate *all* sources of reinforcement to effectively extinguish disruptive behavior. Some teachers work better than others with extinction than others. The extinction technique may be an ineffective strategy for some.

Strategies for Severe Problems and Difficulties with the Inclusion Movement

Disruptive and disabled students are no longer automatically segregated from normal students. The movement in schools toward "inclusion"—which means that all students, regardless of their disabilities, are placed with non-disabled students—has caused mildly disruptive students to be placed in many classrooms.

Do Not Take On Severe Problems Alone: Get Help and Have a Plan

A teacher should not be expected to deal with extreme cases of disruptive behavior *alone*, especially those that are destructive or violent or those that may stem from neurological or psychological disorders. In many schools, support staff and behavioral specialists have been placed in classrooms to assist teachers with disruptive students. Severe or persistent problems with offensive language may require the intervention of additional staff. Novice teachers may need additional help with disruptive students until they gain more experience.

Call for assistance when you perceive that you need it. The school should have additional psychologists and counselors who can be summoned for severe problems experienced during the school day. It is better to have too much assistance in these matters as opposed to too little. With the inclusion of students with behavior and attention problems, the classroom can become very confrontational and even threatening. Some students will yell or curse at other students. They may threaten teachers or refuse to control their own behavior or calm down when told to do so.

When disruption occurs, be prepared. Ask the aide to step in and work with the student one-on-one. Send the student to the principal with a monitor. Take the student to the principal or response team yourself after you have another teacher or aide to watch your class. Know the alternative resources available to you. Check with a fellow teacher who might be able to monitor your class in an emergency.

In extreme cases, a personal aide may need to be hired for a disruptive student, or the student may have to be taught at home by a tutor. There are a variety of options to deal with disruptive students in order to do what is best for the teachers, classmates, students, and parents involved.

Administrators and teachers are still learning how to make inclusion most effective, and no teacher or support staff member should be afraid to ask for help when it is needed. The staff should meet as a group and decide what works first. Classroom aides are extremely helpful if the budget supports their use. An aide should stay with a class of students, not with the classroom. If the aide moves with the class, inclusion and disruptive students can establish a relationship with them, and the aide can better deal with particular students' habits and problems.

Summary

Some students curse to get negative attention from teachers and classmates. Negative attention can be extinguished or punished. Some students have severe behavioral problems which require special attention and additional staffing. Anticipate severe problems and be prepared. Ask others for help when you need it.

CHAPTER 29

Identity Crises
and Authority Problems

First, we want to focus on the relationship between students and the teacher. Students in middle school have already learned that students and teachers have different roles. Teachers are perceived as authority figures, and students expect them to be fair, intelligent, honest, and in control. Teachers who do not live up to these perceptions undermine their own authority. As students enter the adolescent period, they stop accepting everything the teachers say, and they begin to question and challenge adults in positions of authority.

Challenging authority is necessary for many students as challenges and confrontations can provide information about right versus wrong, morality, living in a civilized culture, and getting along with others who are different. A teacher knows he or she will be challenged on a daily basis. A teacher's inconsistent behavior, rules, or language are closely scrutinized and pointed out.

Understand Why Students Develop Identity Problems

Having discussed identity and authority problems between students and teachers, we move on to students' personal identity problems. At this age, students turn their attention toward peer

Cursing is a natural reaction to many identity problems experienced by older students.

relationships. Peers' opinions become more important than a teacher's. All students go through a period of developing and experimenting with different roles as they leave childhood and enter adolescence. For some the transition is smooth and not problematic, but for others it is difficult, confusing, and traumatic.

Students can develop negative relationships with the teacher and with other students that become the source of conflicts in the classroom and off campus. This group of alienated students with negative identities and those with identity crises are likely to use dirty words at school. Half of the teacher's problem is understanding why these identity problems arise, and the other half is knowing what to do when students use curse words. Here are some of the common conflicts and some possible solutions to identity and authority problems.

Strategies for Helping Isolated and Alienated Students

The basic problem with alienated students is a lack of intimacy with other students. Alienated students do not interact with their peers, and they avoid situations where social interaction is required; thus, they become the target for insults and name calling because of their isolation. Alienated students have no deep relationships and rarely talk with classmates. Deep alienation based on psychological trauma may be difficult to overcome.

Break the Cycle

For less affected students with minor alienation difficulties, get them working with a small group and setting realistic goals to break the cycle of alienation.

Talk to the Class

You may need to talk to the alienated student's classmates about his or her problems and try to get the others to be understanding and sympathetic. However, sometimes the plan backfires, and the other students end up picking on, or stigmatizing, the alienated student. You have to assess how your class might react before you ask others for help.

Understanding and Helping Students with Negative Identities (No Intimacy)

Here is a case in which a student has chosen an identity that is anti-social or hostile. The student's problem of establishing an identity is solved when he or she makes a commitment to emulate members of a hostile and negative group.

Minimize the Probability of Acting Out

Negative and hostile students lash out at fellow students and teachers. These outbursts are part of what a negative student thinks he or she has to do to fit the misfit role. Try to eliminate outbursts.

Minimize Interpersonal Challenges to Negative Students

Challenging, confronting, insulting, or picking on such students escalates rather than ameliorates the cursing. Get them focused on performance goals and outcomes and try to minimize challenges to the negative students' egos or attitude problems.

Find the Reinforcers

One strategy is to determine what is reinforcing the negative personality. If these students are getting attention for being deviant, the attention must be eliminated (as in extinction and ignoring). If the deviant behavior is extreme or violent, then this extreme behavior must be eliminated or punished immediately. Change the behavior from negative to positive through CBT (see Part Five).

Understanding "Normal" Identity Crises: On the Path to Adulthood

Most teenagers are seeking normal intimacy status by (a) accepting stereotypical and shallow male or female roles without sexual intimacy, (b) developing sexual relationships without real intimacy, or (c) developing real, mature intimate relationships with long-term sexual commitments. However, first teens must resolve identity problems before they achieve mature intimate relationships experienced in adulthood.

Understanding Four General Identity Crises

Identity crises begin when students examine and question authority, attitudes, beliefs, and values that they took for granted from their parents and teachers. Students begin to seek out values that they can accept and use in everyday situations. Some students become confused and experiment with many different values before settling down; some students blindly or romantically accept classical ideals or parental value systems without questioning the values. The problem students are those students who identify with deviant and negative (to society) values. In general, you should accept identity confusion as a normal part of adolescent development. Understanding the kinds of crises children experience may be helpful to understand why conflicts lead to cursing.

Identity crises have four basic solutions, and some are more successful than others. One group of students experiences no crisis at all by blindly accepting, or committing to, the values and behavior of their parents. These "foreclosers" may be committed without questioning these opinions and values. These students have foreclosed the identity problem without crisis.

Most students, in contrast to the foreclosers, experience some crisis with authority figures and the rules, beliefs, attitudes, and values of the adult generation. Some of these students resolve the crisis by making a commitment to behave and think like some socially acceptable segment of society. "Committed" students have a crisis until they make the commitment. After the commitment, their behavior begins to stabilize.

A third group experiences the identity crisis yet still remains confused. These students continue to experiment with different roles and identities without making a commitment to one identity or another. "Confused" students have crisis without commitment to any identity. Until they make a commitment, their behavior remains unstable.

Finally, there are those students who have no crisis and no commitment. The "uncommitted" students have not locked onto their parents' values. In fact, they have not committed to any values and their identity remains diffuse, and the conflicts remain unresolved.

Summary

Cursing is a natural reaction to many identity problems experienced by students. Cursing allows the student to express youthful angst and frustration. It enables the students to challenge authority figures and test the rules. Cursing helps students to distance themselves from out-groups and bond with in-group members. Understand that individuals thrive on different reinforcers and identify with both good and bad role models. Reach out to alienated, antisocial, and isolated students. Do not overuse competition. Try to eliminate name calling and acting out. Students with long-term, severe problems may need professional help.

CHAPTER 30

Our Changing Language Values

Having read Part Two, you are aware that language values differ from place to place. Language values also change over time. The older one gets, the more we notice that younger speakers use language differently than older ones. Each generation has a new set of experiences influencing language. The goal of this chapter is to inform you what causes our language values to change.

The World before 1960

If you were an adult before 1960, you were exposed to a much more restricted media environment than we have in the 1990s. Adults in the 1950s and early 1960s had conservative television, movies, popular music, news reports, and clothing. Behavior at school was highly regulated. Hair was clean and short. Girls' skirts were long. However, many facets of American life shifted in the mid to late 1960s.

A combination of social changes in this time period led to more liberal values. The Vietnam War protests, civil rights demonstrations, summer race riots, creation of the film rating system, The Beatles and Rolling Stones, political assassinations, coverage of the war on television, clothing styles, and First Amendment freedoms combined, over the years, to create less conservative and more open and explicit means of communication. Adults raised before these

Students must know when and where they have to use conventional language and be capable of communicating with conventional language when it is required.

influences have more conservative views on language than children born after the Vietnam War do.

Other Factors That Change Language Values

Anonymity

If you live in a small town, plenty of people can monitor and respond to your language on a personal level. However, if you live in a large city, you see and speak with people you will never meet again. Under conditions of anonymity, people can use offensive language to express anger, for example, without any repercussions. Speaker anonymity allows one to disrespect people without recourse or retaliation. The more our society shifts away from group cohesion and group effort toward an isolated, individualized lifestyle, the more one can speak and do what one wants without worrying about retaliation.

Language Desensitization

Many of us raised in the 1960s can recall that the word "sucks" was a pretty bad word and semantically referred to oral sex. Today, the same word has lost its clout and means that something is bad, as in "The movie sucked." Adults in their forties and fifties react with a wince to hearing the word, but for children today the word is acceptable. Offensive language is used widely in television and advertisements. Words, through use and over-use, lose some of their power. Once slang terms enter the mass media, they lose the power to offend that they once had. In prime time television, words are frequently used that were forbidden in the 1950s: "bitch," "slut," "whore," "nigger," "queer," "pussy," "homo," "fag," "ass," and "asshole."

Times change, etiquette changes, and words lose their power. Most of us would find the Victorian restrictions on words like "limb," "leg," or "breast" to be quite silly by today's standards. The process by which words lose power is not so much based on a lowering of standards as on the overuse of once-powerful speech.

Daily Hassles

Modern life is stressful, not so much by cataclysmic events but by numerous daily hassles. Waiting in line, finding a parking space, solicitations on the phone, getting stuck in traffic, and scheduling too many events in too short of a time span can all mount up at the end of the day. The stress comes from the accumulation of multiple daily hassles rather than overwhelming life events. Daily hassles combined with anonymity almost guarantee that strangers get angry and curse at other strangers.

Changing Role of Women

Modern women live more public lives than ever before. Women represent a larger portion of those entering in the workplace and a larger segment of managerial positions than before. In many cases, women who must exert power and expertise use strong language in the workplace and at home. The changing role of women has changed the type of language that women hear and use. It is common to hear women cursing in public, and the words women use are becoming more like the offensive words that were exclusively used by men in the past.

Secularization

Many of the laws that restricted and controlled human behavior and communication were set forth by the church. Over the centuries, however, the control of behavior has shifted away from religious bodies to the courts and government. It is obvious that the role of religion and the power of the church in American life has declined over recent years. Religion plays a less significant role in the life of the average American and religion exerts less and less influence on American business and popular culture. With the secularization of control over human communication, language restrictions (on blasphemy, for example) that in the past were strictly enforced by the church have relaxed.

Changing Values and Trends

The momentum for control of human conduct through religious and secular forces swings back and forth like a pendulum. When life becomes too chaotic and meaningless, people tend to shift back to more spiritual supports to justify their actions in daily life. We see these conservative versus liberal trends in religion, politics, and in educational practices. We have recently experienced a period of liberal standards in the 1960s and 1970s which was followed by a conservative backlash in the 1980s.

This book is, in part, a response to the widespread use of offensive language in modern society. More importantly, the increasing use of offensive language is troublesome for teachers and students alike. Even though students may fail to see the need for a working knowledge of conventional speech without cursing, teachers must prepare students to communicate with appropriate language.

Teach the Value of Language Standards

Make Values Functional and Real

Sell good language habits to students. Make good language functional for them. Convince students that good speech (rather than bad speech) functions to give students access to the workplace, higher education, and upper social strata. Describe to students how anonymity, desensitization, values, stress, and cultural shifts affect speech usage.

Show Students that Language Choices Affect the Way They Are Perceived

We form impressions of others and make decisions about people based on the way they look and the way they talk. Bad language leads to bad impressions. This does not mean that a student needs to talk politely and guardedly all the time, but students must know when and where they have to use conventional language and be capable of communicating with conventional language when it is required.

Summary

Teachers should understand that language is always in flux. New jargon appears daily, and words become obsolete. There are social and cultural forces in our country that also change the use of language. The relaxation of media standards, the changing role of women, daily stress and hassles, depersonalization, and anonymity are some of the variables that contribute to an increase in the use of offensive language in everyday life. Overuse of some offensive words by younger speakers desensitizes them to the words that older teachers find unacceptable. Older students may appreciate a classroom discussion on the topic of changing language values. Use some of the material on role models in chapters 19 and 26.

PART FIVE

Implementing Standards to Eliminate Cursing

CHAPTER 31

What Is Cognitive-Behavior Training?

In the modern classroom, teachers take on many different roles. Teachers are role models, behavior managers, problem solvers, instructors, tutors, psychologists, and friends in the eyes of students. Controlling cursing emphasizes two teacher roles: the manager and the instructor.

Primarily, the teacher is a behavior manager of cursing when this unacceptable behavior is to be eliminated. As manager, the teacher manipulates student behavior through reinforcement and punishment, motivating students to achieve self-control. Teachers' actions must be swift, accurate, and consistent. The manager role has to coexist with a teacher's more natural tendency to instruct, give advice, and inform students.

Several kinds of cursing require instruction, rather than behavior management. When children get frustrated and blurt out angry epithets, the teacher needs to first understand why the children are so emotional and then instruct them to express anger with acceptable alternatives.

In brief, sometimes behavior management is the primary technique but in other situations, instruction prevails. Cognitive-behavior training (CBT), as the term suggests, emphasizes management of unacceptable behavior. Instructional strategies are

We aim to change the way students think about language and the way students use language.

used to inform students about alternative as opposed to habitual modes of expression.

The purpose of cognitive-behavior training is to increase desirable behavior and to eliminate unwanted behavior. CBT works by changing students' thoughts and their behavior. New thoughts are implanted in the students' memory banks. New kinds of behavior are acquired and then strengthened, replacing old, inappropriate habits.

Communication skills are transferred from teachers to students through a number of techniques discussed in this part of the book. In the case of dirty word usage, we replace a student's use of dirty language with more appropriate forms of expression. We aim to change the way students think about language and the way students use language.

Our technique is called cognitive-behavior training because it involves teaching the student a rule or strategy that is committed to memory. The rule or strategy becomes a part of the student's problem solving abilities or his or her *cognitions.* By learning to replace improper language with appropriate language, the student and the teacher build more competent or effective communication skills. Because these communication skills are one part of our higher mental processes, they are referred to as cognitive skills. We change the students' cognition about speaking at school. Each student learns a specific set of rules about what can and cannot be said at school.

The term behavior is used to focus training on one specific aspect of the student's life: the public and observable language behavior. Behavior is changed by the consequences of the behavior. The old habits and negative behavior, such as offensive forms of cursing, are eliminated through extinction, punishment, or loss of privileges. New, positive kinds of behaviors such as learning to express anger without cursing are substituted through positive reinforcement, attention, and praise.

The process of elimination and substitution is achieved through a student's appreciation of response-cost. The student learns that unwanted behavior must be paid for through punishments or loss of privileges and that desirable behavior is rewarded with attention and praise. Students learn that language usage is monitored and that the use of unacceptable language has a cost.

Training refers to the course (or schedule) of new skill learning through observations, instruction, and the practice of desirable behaviors over time. By the end of a course of training, the cooperative student has learned to think and behave positively through repeated interactions with the teacher. You could say that students was "trained" through your behavior management techniques and cognitive skill instructions.

The Initial Phase of Cognitive-Behavior Training

After consulting your language values and school policies, you can determine how to apply your values through behavior management techniques. Ask yourself a few preliminary questions. What are students saying now that must be changed? How much are students cursing? What is an acceptable target level of cursing? In other words, where are you now, and where do you want to go? Be precise and make a list of students' present negative and positive behavior. Here are some suggestions and pointers.

In the initial phase of training, students need more attention and monitoring than later on. Immature students need more external commands (written rules and oral reminders) to keep them on track. As students mature and adjust to the rules, they begin to internalize and sub-vocalize (say to themselves silently) the rules of proper speech. The students' silent self-supervision replaces your constant monitoring, controlling, and oral commands. In the beginning, you control the students' behavior, but through training, the student learns to control him or herself. Control of students' behavior and anticipation of potential student problems are two of the keys to success.

Control the Environment and You Control the Behavior in It

To train students, teachers must control students' attention and behavior in class. You must be aware of what conditions in the classroom reinforce the use of dirty language (peer and teacher attention or praise) and eliminate these reinforcers. Before classes begin, anticipate potential conflicts. Take note of your seating plan and the way students move about the class. You should be able to monitor (see and respond to) students at all times. You should place students who agitate each other in different parts of the room. Place students who need the most monitoring in the front and center of the class. Make changes in seating and movement patterns if problems arise. Eliminate anticipated problems and change the environment if new problems arise.

Language in Context

Language problems and CBT do not exist in isolation from other behavior in the classroom. The control of speech exists in a context where other behavior is being controlled through general classroom management. Appropriate language use is important, but there are other kinds of behaviors such as physical violence and property damage that may take precedence over language use. For some teachers in urban settings, where physical violence and use of weapons is a daily occurrence, cursing may not receive much attention. Teachers working in a small, affluent schools may find cursing the most offensive behavior around. Whatever the case, teachers must control the most harmful and disruptive behaviors first. These problems may or may not include language. The strategies for controlling language must be consistent for those used to control other undesirable behavior. Do not expect to control language if you cannot control other aspects of student behavior.

The Teacher's Roles: Manager versus Instructor

Manager

The behavior-management aspect of CBT requires teachers to observe and respond to overt language. Cursing, obscenity, and sexual harassment are controlled by your actions such as ignoring, punishing, or withdrawing privileges. As manager, your primary goal is to control language through direct responses or reactions (response-cost). You are not teaching, instructing, telling, or informing; you are managing. Good behavior management is swift, clear, democratic, precise, and unemotional. Just react to the behavior and do not mince words but instead manage behavior.

Good managers do not vacillate, rationalize, get overly emotional, or ignore behavior that must be changed. Managers motivate students to behave by immediately attaching positive and negative consequences to students' actions. Students are held accountable for their actions through consequences applied to their behavior (reward, praise, ignoring or punishment).

Instructor

The instructor role is more congruent with teaching methods. Language training focuses on presenting new information, revising existing language patterns, (language, rules, or patterns of speech) or replacing inappropriate language. Instruction uses modeling, questioning, telling, and discussing language usage. Instruction changes the way students think about the language they use.

The cognitive-behavior methods work when applied in the appropriate manner. You must respond quickly, consistently, accurately, and fairly. CBT does not work if you are inconsistent (punishing some students but not others), inaccurate (punishing the wrong student), overly punitive (punish harshly for accidental use of slang), or if you fail to understand how to use the methods described. An effective training plan is outlined in the next chapter.

Summary

Teachers change students' behavior by changing the way students think about acceptable ways of speaking. Cognitive strategies are based on simple rules or instructions for self-control. Instructions to students must be simple and clear; they deal with the immediate behavior and are consistently adhered to by both parties.

Management is based on teacher-student interactions and controls students' behavior through consequences. Do not make idle threats but instead ignore, extinguish, praise, or punish behavior. Do not make rules that are unenforceable. Remember that if a rule proves to be unworkable, it can be renegotiated. If applied appropriately (consistently, quickly, and accurately), these CBT techniques will eliminate cursing problems in students.

The remainder of Part Five addresses issues that affect language management. Teachers need to read each chapter in Part Five completely prior to putting a final plan into effect.

CHAPTER 32

Developing a Training Plan

The CBT plan is relatively straightforward. First, record the number and types of language problems that are occurring in your classroom. Second, design and implement your CBT plan (record the who, what, and when of each incident and how you reacted). Finally, keep applying the strategies until the language problems disappear. This chapter outlines a plan for ongoing problems in your classroom, assuming the school year has already begun.

The strategy to control student language problems begins before a school year starts. Teachers must anticipate the occurrence of behavior problems. Language problems should be considered a part of general classroom management and control. The most effective teacher is a *proactive* teacher: one who is ready to head off trouble before it occurs. Proactive teachers prevent language problems by creating a clear set of rules and guidelines that are posted and discussed on the first or second day of class. Posted rules can be reread daily. The types of unacceptable behavior are described, and the consequences for breaking the rules are made clear. An example of a misdeed can be given, and the consequence should be described.

Define Language That Is Prohibited

Are you going to make students accountable for mild profanities such as "damn" or "hell"? Or are mildly offensive terms acceptable?

The essence of the program is to teach children a set of cognitive rules and strategies to control their own behavior.

Consult the section on standards (Part Three) before applying CBT in your classroom. These issues are addressed throughout Part Five.

A worksheet in chapter 38 covers potential problems and reactions. On the worksheet you describe when response-costs (consequence) are applied. What about slips? Are students permitted to slip once or twice before punishments begin? It is a good idea to leave some room for slips. Usually a warning is given first, allowing the student to use self-monitoring and self-control. A first warning is sufficient to end problems, generally. However, a second infraction is punished. Will students be given an in-school suspension immediately, or will they have to serve detention at the end of the day? Regardless of when the cost is paid, students are informed immediately about improper behavior. Generally, repeated infractions receive increasingly stronger punishments.

Teachers Must Be Clear and Precise When Describing Rules to Students

You need to establish a hierarchy of response-costs (punishments, loss of privileges, or the use of suspensions) depending on the severity of the infraction. The greater the misbehavior the greater the cost or consequence applied to it.

The hierarchy can be established by school policy and consensus with other teachers. You may want to consider students' opinions, too, by asking them about their perceptions of the consequences. Most schools already have these consequences in place for various offensives (fighting, swearing, lateness, and disruptive classroom behavior). I cover response-costs in chapter 35.

Effective Teacher Strategies

An effective teacher must be ruthlessly consistent, responding to the first few misbehaviors. Responses must be quick. An effective response would occur within seconds of the offending event. Teachers have to be accurate. Reprimand only the guilty parties and not groups of students. Do not punish the entire class if only one student breaks a rule. The training plan begins with a preventative plan for misbehaviors and a set of appropriate consequences for the misbehaviors is described. Anticipatory planning controls classroom behavior from the first few days of the school year.

Written policy statements (student handbooks) for staff, students, and parents regarding obscenity, discrimination, and sexual harassment can be prepared on a school-wide basis and the consequences of severe language problems (and other violations) made clear to all.

A school is not a perfect world. Somewhere down the line, students will test the rules or try to break the rules for a variety of reasons (see Part Four). If rules and consequences break down, then cognitive-behavior training is initiated to restore classroom decorum. The essence of the plan is to teach children a set of cognitive strategies to control their own speech. Cognitive strategies are initiated when language rules are broken.

Getting Down to Business: Outlining a Plan

First, identify the target behaviors you want to control. These are the forms of inappropriate language described according to your priorities. You must be able to name or define the language rule that was broken.

Second, you must be able to identify the target person(s) involved. Do not punish the entire class because you cannot pinpoint the speaker. Exhibit "with-it-ness" to your class: be attentive, keep your eyes open, and anticipate trouble, especially during transitions between activities.

Third, reactions and responses to misbehaviors depend on your rules and on the type of cursing. Consider various options available to control student language. These options are addressed in the remaining chapters of Part Five and on the worksheet provided in chapter 38.

You should examine these alternative techniques to appreciate the nature and scope of language training. You will return to chapter 32 after reading the rest of Part Five and determine which options are most applicable to your classroom.

Making a Baseline Recording

The next phase (after establishing rules and defining unwanted behavior) is to monitor and record the misbehaviors to establish a baseline, that is, how frequently they occur. The best way to take control of undesirable behavior is to become aware of how frequently it occurs. The reduction of these baseline behaviors is a measure of your success. I suggest a simple graph and checklist as found in chapter 38.

First, decide what types of speech you want to control. During the baseline period, you record this speech but do not do anything about it because you are only measuring how often it occurs. The baseline period, prior to CBT, measures the scope and frequency of language problems. The baseline is simply the number of curses that are used in a class over the period of one week.

Do You Really Have a Problem?

The baseline is used to determine if you do or do not have a language problem. It could be that the cursing is so infrequent that it is not worth your attention. Drawing attention to a very minor problem can make the problem worse. Students may feel that they are being unjustly accused of something that is not important and has not been substantiated to be a problem. Or an entire class may feel punished when only one student is causing a problem. Paying attention to a low frequency behavior may make it increase in frequency due to the attention you give it. You may expend a great deal of effort trying to solve a non-problem.

A Case Study

In one school, teachers had the impression that there was a problem with the use of profanity during break times. Before implementing a plan to modify the students' language, they decided to count the number of swear words during each break for an entire week. When they started counting swear words, they found that their perceptions did not match reality. There were only four or five words for the entire population for each day, a rate that was much too low to worry about. Their original concern was unjustified, and the level of cursing did not warrant a change in policy.

Summary

After a baseline is established, you decide if there is a sufficient amount of cursing to warrant a change in policy and procedures. If there is a problem, then the appropriate CBT strategies can be selected. During the use of these strategies, you continue charting what happens in your class. The purpose of charting behaviors (after the baseline period) is to determine if the CBT is having the desired effect, that is, decreasing the cursing. If cursing declines to near zero, you have been successful. If you do not reduce the baseline numbers, you then change your plan and determine what went wrong.

CHAPTER 33

Helping Students Hear
What They Are Saying

Let us assume that classes have begun and the rules you have in place are not working. You now decide to change the students' language and take a baseline measure of it. When you decide to change your students' language, one strategy you may try is to get the students to listen to what they are saying. At this point, you have already recorded (during the baseline phase) what students have been saying and can describe different types of problems (vulgarity, profanity, slang, slurs, and so forth) that are occurring in your class. You can tape-record some speech in non-class contexts (in the hallway, playground, or at lunch).

Self-Monitoring and Self-Awareness

When you have examples of inappropriate language, present them to the class without using the offensive words per se. You can refer to an infraction in general terms. For example, "He used a vulgar term for urinating." The purpose is to get each student to monitor his or her own language. To change a bad habit, you must be aware that you are doing it. Show students what they are saying.

Using the information from Part Two (on values), instruct students why these forms of language cannot be used in the classroom. Focus on the three Rs (reason, respect, and responsibility), federal and state

To change a bad habit, you must be aware that you are doing it.

laws, school policy, and community values. Students should be told that it is your job to help them develop appropriate language skills, so they can get along in mainstream American society. Tell students that the schoolroom is one of the places where they learn about societal expectations and conventional speech.

Guidelines and Strategies

Listen to Others and Observe Consequences

Observational learning or modeling is based on the idea that we learn to communicate by watching others speak and noting how listeners react. Observations cause imitation or suppression. Certainly, joking is based on observation: we hear someone tell a joke and note how listeners respond. A funny joke gets a good response, so we decide to tell the joke (imitating and modeling what we heard), expecting to get a laugh. Observing negative consequences for improper language, however, leads to suppression.

Vicarious Learning

Consider the observational learning which occurs after aggression in the classroom. The class hears a student arguing with obscenities and observes that he or she gets punished by the teacher for doing so. When students observe the obscene speech getting punished, they learn vicariously (without being punished themselves) that the use of obscene speech has dire consequences. They should not repeat the obscenity because they learned that the teacher punishes the use of obscenities.

You could ask students to pay attention to how you control the classroom, but that would be unnecessary because they already pay close attention to teachers' methods and subsequent effects. In addition to the effect of vicarious learning on your students, they also receive concrete descriptions of rules governing their behavior and consequences for misbehavior.

Describe the Consequences of Using Unacceptable Language

Give an example of inappropriate speech and what would happen to the students involved. For example, repeat the following:

When you use an obscenity in my classroom, you will first be
told that you used an obscenity and warned that the next use
will result in an in-school suspension. If you use a second
obscenity, you will be given a suspension during your free time,
during which we will talk about your language.

Monitor and Pay Attention

Suggest that students start paying attention to their own speech
styles and try to eliminate bad habits by helping each other clean up
substandard speech. Students can listen to model speakers and try to
copy the role models. Some of these role models are described in
chapter 26.

You can (if you have a receptive class and the permission of
administrators and parents) tape record the class or videotape your
class and acknowledge the students who are trying the hardest and
changing the most in a positive direction.

Slow Down, Take Turns, Do Not Interrupt

Sometimes the modern classroom has too much going on at
once. Ask students to follow simple rules of language etiquette for
discussions. The classroom is not a street corner or locker room. Ask
students to debate an important topic by following formal rules of
order. Formal debate helps students listen to each other and allows a
teacher time to monitor language more carefully than times when
students talk out of turn.

Only you can determine which of the remaining exercises will
work for your class. Remember that it never hurts to try something
new if you think it has a good chance of being effective.

Diary Keeping

Ask students to keep a language diary and record how they
handle tough situations in an appropriate manner ("I got mad at my
brother but did not call him a name"). Students can report these to
the class. You can also collect their dairies from time to time.

Role Playing

Ask students to role play different communication situations like waiting in a long line at a store, talking to a younger brother or sister about not using dirty words, confronting an angry parent or friend, expressing feelings to a good friend, telling someone that he or she did something wrong, or reading the news for a television broadcast. Role playing is a good way to increase awareness. The practice of handling emotional or socially constrained situations (presenting the news or talking to an authority figure) strengthens good communication skills and decreases students' anxiety about how to respond in stressful situations.

Say It Again, But This Time...

When a student has made a minor language mistake that is not worthy of punishment, such as unnecessary use of slang or vulgarity, ask him or her to rephrase the statement with appropriate language: "Please say that again, but this time without using slang."

Role Model and Copycat

Ask students to select a role model for good language, one who appears on television. They can repeat (copycat) some of the dialogue that impressed them. We do this frequently in school with Shakespeare and Abraham Lincoln, but we need to sample speech from contemporary models whom students admire. It is helpful to present a videotaped speech to show students an example of good speaking skills. Then students have a model for selecting their role models, ones that are acceptable for classroom use.

Summary

Students learn through observation. They can eliminate cursing by monitoring each others' speech, role playing good speaking habits, and learning alternative ways to express emotions. Students should be told the consequences of using bad language and why good speech is necessary to communicate with other educated people.

CHAPTER 34

Using Positive
Behavior Reinforcement

One goal of CBT is to establish a predictable set of desirable behaviors through positive reinforcement. Catch students being good and reinforce their behavior. Positive reinforcement is also given for low rates of undesirable behavior such as completing a class period without using obscenities. Positive reinforcement is easier to use than punishment and other aversive techniques. Positive reinforcement works as well as punishment and carries fewer negative aftereffects.

The Nature of Positive Reinforcement

Positive reinforcement is simply a reward system. Reinforcers and rewards increase the frequency of behavior. Rewards can be tangible or intangible. Tangible rewards are objects such as tokens or stickers that are used to "purchase" privileges. Though tangibles are widely used in schools, I suggest using intangibles because we want students to develop self-motivation and self-control without relying on a material reward. Intangibles are cheaper, easier to administer, and their use promotes internal rather than external motivation.

Intangibles include verbal acknowledgment, praise, presenting a student's language as an example or model to the class, writing a

Positive reinforcement works as well as punishment and carries fewer negative aftereffects.

flattering or supportive note on homework that is returned, access to privileges (activities, free time, or extracurricular work), and grades. In the long run, they are better for students than tangibles because they make students focus on the activity, not the prize.

Rewarding the Elimination of Bad Speech

Rewards can be given for using appropriate speech or for avoiding inappropriate speech. Rewards should be used frequently in the initial phase of CBT. Reward good speakers for expressing themselves with appropriate speech. Reward students who have been cursing, when they eliminate cursing.

Rewarding Appropriate Speech

When you hear a student speaking appropriately, one who has had trouble suppressing foul language, praise him or her for the appropriate speech. Say something simple such as, "I like the way you put that," "You made your point clearly," or "Now you're on the right track." Do not *overpraise*. Some students who are sensitive to how they are perceived by their peers may view too much praise as bad. Sensitive students or those who are teased by peers for being a "good" student may only need a nod of the head or a simple "Good," "That's right," or "Umm-hmm" without the sugar coating.

Praise Must Be Sincere

False praise or undeserved praise is perceived as such and diminishes student effort. Praising students for very minor contributions to the class trivializes the positive value of praise and undermines the overall effect of praising.

Teacher-Student Contracts

You can develop a behavior contract with a student, specifying behavior to be controlled and consequences for controlling behavior. The student writes the contract, and it is subject to teacher approval. Goals need to be reasonable and realistic. The contract might indicate that a reward, such as extra free time, would be received when the student did not swear in class for an entire week.

Contracts are negotiated on an individual basis when a student exhibits language problems. A good time to write a contract is during a suspension period. Allow the student a good deal of freedom in setting the guidelines of the contract. The point is to give the student a sense of self-control and allow him or her to see that positive language is an achievable goal.

Summary

Reinforcements are tangible (stickers or prizes) and intangible (praise, positive comments, and verbal recognition) rewards for the use of appropriate behaviors. Teachers should use reinforcement to increase the frequency of appropriate language. They can also reward students who decrease their use of inappropriate language. Make sure you understand what is reinforcing or rewarding to students. What is rewarding to one student may not necessarily work for another. Praise is an effective reinforcement, but praising too much is not. Student-teacher contracts allow students to determine their own rewards. Through the use of positive reinforcement, we expect students to be accountable for their own behaviors. We do not want students who have to be constantly monitored and evaluated by teachers. Students need to develop a sense of self-control and the ability to monitor speech without the teacher looking over his or her shoulder all the time.

CHAPTER 35

Punishing Effectively and Non-Abusively

Punishment is the application of an aversive consequence to the use of unacceptable speech. A student does something bad, and you do something bad to him or her in response. Punishment is the "cost" of the undesirable behavior. Punishment suppresses behavior more quickly than other forms of CBT, but its use presents some problems for teachers. Suppressed behavior must be accompanied with information about what kinds of positive behavior are needed to replace undesirable types. Otherwise, we end up with suppressed students (like cowering dogs) who lack a sense of self-control and direction. Punishment is the least desirable form of CBT and should be used when positive reinforcement or withholding privileges does not reduce the use of inappropriate speech or with students who have a long record of misbehavior.

Punishment should be used in cases where a student had a *choice* to use appropriate language but chose not to use appropriate speech. Punishment is used when a student is clearly responsible for bad language and has not been pushed into the corner by other circumstances. However, when a student is extremely angry, punishment is not fully effective because the student is focused on the frustrating event. Punishment in this case may escalate some emotional speech rather than eliminate it.

Punishment is used for students who do not respond to alternatives, for extremely offensive speech (sexual harassment,

If you intend to punish a behavior, then punish it. Do not just threaten it.

racial slurs, or obscenities), for students who chronically break the school's rules, and for voluntary language (as opposed to slips or accidents).

Punishment may be more effective for some personality types. Reinforcement and praise do not always work for anti-social and hostile students or those with negative identities. Giving praise or positive reinforcement to chronic misbehavers to change their language may not be perceived as rewarding to them. These tough cases may need to be controlled with response-costs for their behaviors. For example, "You use obscenities, you stay after school."

Effective Punishment

For punishment to be effective, three conditions must be met. Punishment must be delivered immediately to the offending party. Immediate punishment has the effect of suppressing the offender's behavior, and the suppressing effect may "ripple" across the entire classroom.

Second, you must inform the offender what rule has been broken. Make it clear to the student that he or she had a choice and did not take responsibility; therefore, he or she must take the blame and consequence.

Third, for punishment to be effective, the offender must be informed about alternative forms of expression ("You could have said…") that do not include offensive language. When you choose to punish, you choose to inform, as well.

Using Markers

Immediate delivery of punishment may mean that the student receives a "marker" after the second use of forbidden language. A marker could be a colored mark on a chart, a note, or a colored chip. The cost of each marker could be five minutes after-school detention. The behavior is dealt with immediately, and the cost is paid later at the end of the school day.

Effective punishments are realistic consequences applied to clear infractions of rules. Punishment rules are simple: "If you say X, then this (punishment) is what will happen to you." Make it clear that the behavior is being punished and that the behavior is bad, not the person. The bad behavior is to be eliminated, and the student is to be improved.

Assess a Student's Emotional State

Do not punish students when they are so emotional or upset that they cannot listen to you or respond to you in a rational manner. In the case of anger expression, deal with the anger first and the language infraction last. Do not make matters worse by intensifying an already volatile situation.

Do Not Make Idle Threats

Remind students of the classroom rules and remind them of the consequence of breaking the rules. Threats are not necessary but reminders are. If you intend to punish a behavior, then punish it. Do not just threaten it. Be careful that you do not threaten to do something to a student that is outside of your authority such as kick him off the football team or dismiss him from the school. All you must do is state the rule that was broken and state the punishment that is the consequence.

A Teacher's Anger: Control Your Own Emotions during CBT

Do not administer punishments when you are too angry to respond. It is more effective to cool down first and think of your responsibilities and alternatives rather than making a poor judgment. You can always delay punishment, but you cannot change your class's opinion of you if you fly off the handle and lose control, punishing unjustly.

One general problem with punishment is that using it makes a teacher look like a bad role model, like a person who has lost control. You want to make students feel that you are in control. Try positive alternatives first and do not choose punishments when other interventions can work. Losing your temper makes students think that you have lost control. When students think you have lost control, they will try to manipulate you in class in many other ways to get you to lose your cool.

Punishment Protocol and Response-Cost Hierarchy

Before you begin CBT, make a rank-ordered list from mild to strong forms of punishment. Make sure these punishments conform to school policy and past policy. Most schools already have such a protocol for dealing with student conduct problems in a student handbook format or other written policy. Have a fellow teacher read your hierarchy and ask for suggestions or advice about using the punishments you have selected. Here is an example of a response-cost hierarchy or protocol for older middle school students:

- first infraction: warning

- second occurrence: loss of free period or recess time; in-class suspension (timeout)

- third occurrence: in-school suspension, letter to parents, or loss of privileges (sports, drama, or band)

- fourth occurrence: after-school suspension or litter clean-up; work conforming to state laws (some do not permit janitorial duties)

- fifth occurrence: after-school suspension or parent conference; school counselor intervention

- sixth occurrence: deliver student to parent at work or home

I suggest that you do not use extra coursework as a punishment. Doing so gives students the idea that schoolwork is aversive. Do not use corporal punishment or techniques that cause physical pain. Consult school guidelines.

Apologies

Students who have insulted or verbally attacked another student can be made to apologize to the victim. Apologies can be in private or in public and may be either oral or written in nature. Students who have disrupted an entire classroom can be made to apologize to fellow students before resuming normal classroom activities. Making students apologize to victims forces students to deal with their language on a personal basis and makes them take responsibility for their actions. A sincere apology creates a sense of humility and forces a student to consider the effect of language on others.

Reasonable punishments include after-school (AS) and in-school suspension (ISS), campus clean up, campus repairs, or other community service that is ethical and reasonable. During suspensions, you may want to talk to your students about their language problems. Again, this is a good time to develop a contract with students to gain access to rewards as opposed to getting punished again. Students who have been caught writing graffiti can be made to clean up the graffiti and restore or repaint the areas that were damaged. Severe problems are to be brought to the parents' attention and should result in more extensive suspensions until the student's behavior is brought under control.

Summary

Most schools use various kinds of punishment (suspensions or notifying parents) to suppress bad behavior. Effective punishments are quickly and accurately delivered, and afterward students are instructed to use alternative, acceptable forms of behavior. Teachers should be attentive to students' emotional states and their own emotional level before punishing. Use punishments when other forms of behavior management have not been effective.

CHAPTER 36

Withholding Privileges and Counterconditioning

Two effective methods of controlling behavior are through the withdrawal of expected privileges and the conditioning behavior which competes with the undesirable behavior (counterconditioning). These techniques are based on response-cost and can also be considered as more desirable alternatives to punishment. The first section of the chapter addresses withholding privileges, and the last section covers counterconditioning methods.

Withholding

While punishment techniques apply aversive costs (suspension or campus clean-up) to undesirable behavior, withholding techniques control students by taking something desirable (free time, extracurricular activities with sports, drama, or music groups) away from them until they behave. Withholding a privilege occurs when a student uses inappropriate speech. For example, a student who uses an obscenity in class is not permitted to attend an upcoming school dance. Students can be denied privileges for a given period of time or until they acquire acceptable speech patterns; then the access to privileges is restored.

Withholding techniques are forms of "escape" learning. Students escape from the denial of privileges by being good. A good example

Complete loss of privileges is a good alternative to punishments.

of withholding a privilege might be as follows: students are permitted to listen to a radio in the lunchroom. If any bad language occurs, the radio is turned off. If no bad language is used the rest of the day, the radio will be turned on at lunchtime the next day. The students lose the access to the music, but they escape the silence by eliminating bad language.

Permanent loss of privileges operates as effectively as punishment. However, as mentioned above, loss of privileges is not punishment because the loss is not an aversive consequence. Withholding is the loss of an expected, positive consequence. Complete loss of privileges is a good alternative to punishments and should be considered as a replacement for punishment. Permanent or extended loss of privilege, in line with the previous example, would occur when students have used foul language in the lunchroom for several days and show no sign of responding to temporary losses. Consequently, the radio is removed and never returned during the school year.

Counterconditioning

Counterconditioning is the reinforcement of behavior that is incompatible with undesirable behaviors. For example, counting to ten slowly is incompatible with yelling and expressing anger. Making students speak positively about another student is incompatible with name calling. Counterconditioning substitutes a desirable or positive behavior for an undesirable behavior. Since the student cannot say two different sentences at once, substituting the desirable behaviors stamps out the undesirable ones. Over time, acceptable behaviors increase and unacceptable ones decrease.

Rewarding Speech Patterns Incompatible with Talking Dirty

Several manners of speaking eliminate cursing because they are incompatible with cursing. By using euphemisms, sarcastic irony, and positive statement emphasis, you can allow students to express negative statements in an acceptable and inoffensive way.

Accentuate the Positive First

With this strategy, students are permitted to make an appropriate negative statement, but they must state a positive view first. For example, assume one student steps on another's foot while standing in line. The student would say, "I know that you did not mean to step on my foot, but that hurt."

Students are urged to say a positive statement before any negative statements are made. If one student disputes what another has said, he or she would have to say something like, "I know you have the right to express your own opinion, but I do not agree with what you are saying."

Students should be given several examples of accentuating the positive first. If you think that a student wants to express anger, call another student a name, or make an insensitive remark, you tell the student "Positive first" as you are calling on him or her. The "positive first" strategy is difficult for middle school students, but mature and sensitive students see the advantages of doing it.

Euphemisms Are Acceptable

We are all familiar with euphemisms, words and phrases that are the acceptable equivalents of taboo or offensive counterparts. Euphemisms are used so frequently in colloquial speech that you may not be aware of them. Euphemisms are especially helpful substitutes for expressing anger. Here are a few euphemisms with dysphemisms in parentheses: "darn" ("damn"), "sugar" or "shoot" ("shit"), "fudge" or "fooie" ("fuck"), "jeez" or "jeeps" ("Jesus"), "cripes" or "crimony" ("Christ"), "godfrey daniels" or "gosh darn" ("goddamn"), "heck" ("hell"), and the list goes on.

Euphemisms are certainly acceptable replacements for physical violence or aggression. They are acceptable to mainstream culture as expressions of anger, and they are used widely in print and mass media. Students can be told that these are acceptable terms for the classroom if the use of euphemisms do not violate school policy.

Sarcasm or Sarcastic Irony

Sarcasm occurs when a stated opinion is the opposite of the intended meaning. For example, a student spills glue on the desk and says something like, "That was very nice," "What a nice desk I have," or "I really like making messes." Sarcasm defuses emotions and makes light of the behavior in question.

Sarcasm is incompatible with anger because it is a form of humor. When a student is angry, he or she would have to say "Now that made me really happy" or "What a great day I am having." Students who are impulsive or emotional may benefit most from sarcasm. However, sarcasm may not work with those students who do not have good language or verbal skills.

While most parents and novice teachers can easily figure out how to use punishments, alternative management strategies may take some study time. You will find that many of the alternatives described above are just as effective as punishment.

Summary

Withholding privileges (removing a desired or expected reward) and counterconditioning (establishing positive behavior that competes with and replaces negative behavior) are effective alternatives to using punishments. Withholding teaches students to monitor their own behavior and develop self-control. Various counterconditioning techniques provide students with acceptable alternative methods of expressing strong emotions without resorting to cursing language.

CHAPTER 37

Establishing Suspension Procedures

Most schools have developed suspension policies. I review some strategies here as they apply to controlling episodes of cursing.

Timeout or In-Class Suspension

The use of timeout for disruptive behavior is common practice in many elementary school settings. As students age, timeout is used less frequently. Teachers who decide to use in-class suspension (ICS) should decide what types of behavior result in the use of ICS. Fighting, pushing, hitting, chasing, teasing, cursing, name calling, and making disruptive noises during class are examples of behavior that may result in an in-class suspension. Note that the timeout is not a punishment. It is used to allow a student to settle down and regain self-control before returning to his or her seat.

A suspension area can be prepared in the classroom, given sufficient space and supervision, with a desk facing away from the class and supplied with a few books or writing materials. Students are expected to continue class work during this period and reflect on why they are in timeout. The teacher does not debate the misdeed in question or lecture students about the misbehavior. When the child

An effective school already has prepared by the first day of class a written policy for students and parents that specifies what type of conduct or manners are expected.

reaches the suspension area he/she remains there until the emotion subsides. A standard time or duration is not set. The student returns when ready. In-class suspension works best with young students.

An effective school already has prepared by the first day of class a written policy for students and parents that specifies what type of conduct or manners are expected. When discussing timeout or suspension, describe the timeout procedure to students and tell them it is used to allow them to calm down and reflect. Tell students where the suspension area is and what to do when you say "suspended." Inform students what to do during suspension and what to do when the suspension is over. Also describe what happens if they do not go directly and promptly (within one minute) to the suspension area.

Repeated occurrences of misbehavior and defiant behavior, like when students do not go to suspension, result in the use of an extended suspension known as "in-school suspension."

In-School Suspension

One time-honored suspension is to send the offending student to the principal's office. If he or she can be trusted, the offender can go to the office alone, but for troublesome offenders an aide or another student may be required to make sure the student actually goes to the office. Schools also use more extensive suspensions within the school. An extended timeout or in-school suspension (ISS) takes place in a different, isolated area of the school and may last from one half an hour to three hours. The extended timeout area needs to have a toilet facility and a place for the students to eat lunch or a snack when those events are included in the extended in-school suspension. There must be a teacher or timeout assistant who monitors but does not talk to the children in timeout about their misdeeds. Students are not sent alone but always with at least one other student and at least one adult.

After-School Suspension

The after-school suspension (AS) can be given when the ISS is impossible due to the student's schedule or room availability. It is best not to take students out of class for ISS as this may amount to a negative reinforcement (getting out of the aversive classroom by acting bad). AS can last long enough for the student to miss his or her ride home (ten to fifteen minutes) to an hour. Parents should be notified by phone or with a letter.

Students can be asked to stay in a designated area or to help clean up litter in a room or a hallway with adult supervision. Students can be required to attend the teacher-supervised after-school suspension. They can be asked to engage in a writing exercise that forces them to account for their behavior and to suggest a behavior contract for better behavior and potential rewards for the reduced usage of offensive language or increases in positive language. Students can use this time to complete schoolwork.

These suspension procedures must be considered in light of school policy and state laws. States vary with respect to what students can be asked to do during a suspension (clean up) and on days of the week suspension can occur (Saturday).

Summary

Most schools use different types of suspensions to punish undesirable behavior. Suspensions can range in severity from brief in-class timeouts for minor infractions to extended after-school sessions where assignments are completed. Teachers should consult school policies regarding the use of suspensions.

CHAPTER 38

Charting Language Change

This chapter presents the three stages in designing and carrying out a language plan. The first stage is to determine what language problems exist at your school and to anticipate how you would respond to each type of problem with the CBT strategies (reward, punishment, ignoring, or suspension) suggested previously. The second stage is to record a baseline, indicating the frequency of the problems in your classroom over the course of a week. The third stage is to chart the effect of CBT on the problem language. Begin with making decisions about language problems and CBT strategies.

Worksheet 4: Outlining Your Plan

Throughout the book, I have asked you to determine what language problems you experience, and in Part Five I described alternative strategies you can choose to respond to a given problem. You must make judgments about problems and strategies based on your experience and your particular context. You can make these judgments on Worksheet 4. You will notice that this worksheet is similar to Worksheet 3; however, now you have to decide what strategies you will apply to each type of problem. As discussed previously, you also have to decide what language is acceptable and what types of language are unacceptable. At this point, you should complete Worksheet 4 in as much detail as possible. It will become the outline of your plan. You will get another chance to work with problems or responses in Part Six.

Outline a plan. Record a baseline. Record data during CBT.

Worksheet 4: Problems and Responses

Fill out the response sections in detail. Use additional paper if necessary. Compare your worksheet to other teachers' when completed.

1. Unacceptable Language   My Response:

a. sexual harassment
(e.g., "nice tits,"
"Jane is a slut,"
harassing graffiti,
other harassment issues)

b. gender or racial
discrimination (e.g.,
"nigger," "Sam is
a queer," "jew bastard,"
other racial language)

c. violations of school
policy regarding language
(consult school handbook;
examples: "Coed Naked"
or offensive clothing,
profanity on the school
bus, "fuck you," other
violations)

d. other language
problems (cite specific
cases; examples: slang,
scatology, profanity,
name calling)

2. Inappropriate Language You Will Tolerate
(e.g., "sucks," "puke"; list others)

My Response:

3. Proactive/Preventive Strategies for First Day of School
(e.g., rules, posters)

My Response:

Recording a Baseline

Once you have worked out on Worksheet 4 what problems you anticipate, you can begin counting them during the baseline period. If you have one class for the entire day, your task is simple. Record the total number of word types for the entire day. If you have different classes, you should record a different baseline for each class. Tabulate cursing each day for an entire week.

What to Record?

A simple strategy is to classify language problems as either unacceptable (U) and inappropriate (I). The "unacceptable" category includes harassment, discrimination, and obscenity. The "inappropriate" category includes name calling, profanity, scatology, and other language sanctioned in school policies. This U versus I strategy serves to separate severe problems from milder violations of school policy. You could combine all violations into one category or record a baseline for each category in Part One, but using U/I is easiest.

The following chart can be copied and used to plot your data during both baseline and CBT phases.

Baseline and CBT Word Frequency Chart

DATE/CLASS	SPEAKER	TARGET(S)	CURSE WORD(S)	STRATEGY RESPONSE

Classroom Language Data Log

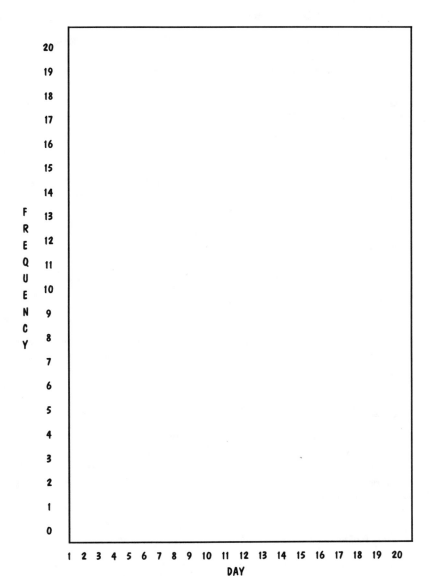

Using the Classroom Language Data Log

Recording Data During CBT

The Classroom Language Data Log on the previous page is designed to record individual episodes of cursing language. You can use this during your baseline period, although you do not fill in the "response" portion. Otherwise, the log is used during your CBT plan to keep a record of the speaker, the language, and your response or the strategy employed to control the cursing in question. Here is how it works.

Date or Class

Record the particular date or indicate a particular class on a date. Segregating data for different classes is important when different language problems occur for one group but not for others.

Speaker

Enter the initials of the student who has uttered the curse word.

Target

If the curse was spoken to a "target" or victim, record the initials of the target. If there was no target, as when a speaker is frustrated and blurts out an epithet, record "0," meaning no target.

Curse Words

Indicate the specific words used ("Fuck you" or "Go to hell"). Details are important, but you may not have time to write down a detailed recording of every word that a student used. Record the language as soon as possible and do not rely on your memory, especially if you are not recording the data on tape.

Your Response

What did you do after the cursing? Did you ignore, warn, threaten, speak to the class, speak to the speaker, punish, withhold privileges, or suspend? Record your reaction to the student according to the particular strategy discussed earlier. During the baseline period, you do not respond to these events, but you merely record their frequencies. During CBT, you do respond and record your management techniques or responses to each cursing episode.

When and How to Record

You can keep the log on your desk or in a notebook to be filled in as soon as possible after the event occurs. It is important during the baseline phase of CBT that the students do not know what you are doing. Students might curse more frequently if they think you are recording what each of them is saying.

During the course of CBT, you (or your aide) can log the episodes as they happen. As the students quickly learn that there are consequences for cursing, they learn that you are recording what they are saying. You need the frequency of occurrence data if you are going to make contracts with students for low frequency of cursing language. Even if you do not have a behavior contract with a student, you can use these frequency data to praise students for not cursing. You also have an account of those students who have been warned (and might be punished upon the next instance).

Adding Up the Data: Categories or Words

I suggest that you sort words into categories of Unacceptable and Inappropriate. You could also use categories (profanity, scatology, harassment, and so forth) if you like. Your sorting depends on the variety of language you are hearing and what kinds of details are important.

Charting the Baseline and CBT Frequencies

Sum up each category from your Classroom Language Data Log for each class each day. Enter the frequency (0-20) on the Frequency Chart. Your data might look like that on the next page.

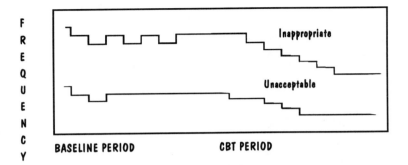

During the baseline period, the frequencies will bounce up and down a little bit but basically remain fairly stable, resulting in straight lines. During an effective CBT plan, these frequencies begin to decrease, and the lines will staircase downward to near zero, indicating the efficacy of CBT (as mentioned earlier). As the frequency of problem behavior decreases, you know that you have a good, effective plan.

Different types of language occur at different rates. Generally, strong speech is used less frequently than mild speech. Notice that we expect less offensive inappropriate language (profanity, scatology, and slang) to occur at a higher rate than more offensive unacceptable language (harassment, obscenity, or racial slurs). As such, the two lines representing inappropriate versus unacceptable language are somewhat parallel. The assumption is that both will decrease during the course of the CBT.

Summary

Charting and controlling bad language at school occurs over three stages. First, problem behaviors are defined and effective responses to them are selected. Next, a baseline, indicating the frequency of bad speech, is recorded, and afterwards you determine if there is a problem and what kind of plan is required. Finally, a CBT plan is developed and applied to the problem behavior. The effect of the plan on the behavior is determined by recording the frequencies of different types of offensive language during the implementation of the plan. When frequencies decline, you have been successful.

CHAPTER 39

What If Things Go Wrong?

An effective, proactive teacher anticipates student behavior patterns and prepares for them. You may start off the school year with the anticipation of a variety of student behaviors. You can plan for good behavior and for problems in the classroom and thus devise a set of rules and guidelines to deal with recurrent and predictable management problems from day one. Let us assume that somewhere in the middle of the year, things go wrong, and your rules are not working. Here are some suggestions for you in the event that your class does not behave as anticipated.

Examine Your Original Expectations and Initial Plans and Rules for Dealing with Problems

Decide if the original CBT plan is defective. Maybe you are using too much punishment, administering punishment inconsistently, giving too much attention to attention seekers. or picking on the wrong students. Maybe you are not administering the CBT in the appropriate manner.

Reexamine Your CBT

Check on your baseline scores and look at increases or decreases in specific types of cursing. Did you lose control of slang but subdue obscenity? Did you maintain control for a period of time but lose

Replace the rules that are not working and those that are unnecessary.

control after a vacation? Maybe you just need to adhere to the original plan. Behavior modification, as in CBT, works when used properly.

Redesign Your Rules

Replace the rules that are not working and those that are unnecessary. Rules should be clear and concise. Maybe you had a rule prohibiting the use of slang. You later realize that students have never been taught the use of clinical or acceptable terms for sexual behavior or body parts and cannot talk about these matters without using slang and vulgarity. Obviously, you need to permit the use of non-clinical language in these matters until the students are taught a more acceptable lexicon.

Enlist the Help of Other Teachers

Find a teacher who has handled the problem of students using dirty words effectively in the past and ask how he or she did it. Ask for advice, giving specific details of your classroom disruptions.

Is It You or the School?

Determine if the problem of incivility and the use of bad language is school wide. If other teachers do not have similar problems, then focus on your own methods of training. You and others may need assertive training. A refresher course in classroom management skills may be warranted and helpful. Determine if you are doing anything to provoke bad language unintentionally.

It may be possible that you think you are ignoring and extinguishing profanities when you may be actually paying attention to them and increasing their frequency. Perhaps your punishment is inconsistent. Are you punishing the wrong people? Are you inconsistent, rewarding one day and not the next?

Get In-Service Training if the Problem Is School-Wide

The entire staff may need a bit of retraining to deal successfully with the language problem if several teachers are having similar problems.

Set Up a Student-Led Mediation Board for Dispute Resolution

Make sure that bad language is a behavior that is addressed in disputes between students and between students and teachers. Eliminate insults and taunts that occur in other forms of disputes like arguing or fighting. There are several good books available for peer mediation of conflicts.

Severe problems, once identified, should be handled elsewhere. Students with legal, psychological, or home-based problems may need counseling or help that is outside of your control or expertise. School systems without adequate counseling staff may not be able to alleviate the problems of some students.

Remember Your Priorities

Your first job is to educate students through instruction. Taking on the role of parent, counselor, probation officer, or priest is not a primary duty and taking on these roles wear you down.

A Quick Checklist

I would like to end this part of the book with a checklist outlining ways to change classroom language.

Before School Begins

- Consult with interested administrators and teachers about developing or updating a set of policies regarding language and language values in the context of other behaviors that are unacceptable. Decide what must be controlled in the classroom. Decide what is acceptable outside of the classroom.

- Examine policies regarding in-school suspensions, after-school suspensions, and in-class suspensions (timeouts). Make decisions about when and how to suspend students.

- Examine what privileges can be withdrawn from students who curse.

- Decide how many warnings you will give students before punishing them or taking away their privileges.

- Prioritize the elimination of sexual harassment, discrimination, and obscenity.

- Devise a written policy about unacceptable behavior for staff, students, and parents.

- Check your roster and anticipate problem students from previous years. Consult with successful teachers regarding how to handle some of these problem cases. Identify students with long-term personality, social, identity, authority, negative attention-seeking, gang affiliation, role model, or family problems.

- Examine your room arrangement and eliminate problem areas.

- Pick a small set of language rules and consequences that will be presented on the first few days of class.

- Decide what consequences you will apply to unacceptable student behavior.

Once Classes Start

- Remind the class that your first responsibility is to teach them and that you have the right and responsibility to control any behavior that interferes with learning.

- Tell students the cursing rules. Give out the written policy. Describe the costs of cursing in the written policy, too.

- Be prepared to chart cursing. Copy the charts in chapter 38.

- React immediately to incidents of harassment, discrimination, or obscenity.

- Do not overreact, overpraise, punish the entire class when one student is at fault, or punish the wrong person.

- Ignore minor infractions.

- Give a warning before you punish.

- Find the cause of anger and take care that you do not escalate anger.

Be Positive

- Praise students who are good language users.

- Point out good role models, especially students' "heros."

Point Out the Consequences of Bad Language

- Use famous people in media who got into trouble for cursing.

- Indicate how cursing limits students' abilities to get good jobs or respect, to speak in public, and to be perceived as educated people.

When Things Go Wrong

- Reexamine your rules. Are your priorities realistic?

- Reexamine the efficacy of your CBT methods. Are you consistent? Are you ignoring, praising, reinforcing, and punishing effectively?

- Consult with an effective teacher.

- Schedule a problem solving or brainstorming session with other teachers.

Summary

Be prepared for things to go wrong. Make sure your CBT plan and strategies are appropriate. Change what is not working. Have a plan that covers the entire year from before school starts until it ends. Determine if language problems are school-wide. You may need some in-service programs to bolster behavior management approaches and bad language programs.

PART SIX

Coping with Specific Problems

CHAPTER 40

Dealing with Obscenity and Severe Problems

Start with prevention. Schools must have a clearly written policy regarding unacceptable conduct. Illegal conduct and that which interferes with the school's primary responsibility of instructing students should be clearly specified. The policy states the types of punishments and sanctions (loss of privileges, in class suspension, in-school suspension, after-school suspension, notification of parents, or dismissal) that teachers and administrators can use. Every teacher and student should have a copy of these rules. Students should be encouraged to take the policies home and discuss the handbook with parents. Time should be devoted for a review of these rules in class. Every school must have a clear statement about obscenity, harassment, and discrimination. Although the use of obscenity is not criminal behavior, most schools define the use of obscene speech as unacceptable and develop policies to eliminate bad language on campus.

Obscenity and What to Do About It

Obscenities are the most offensive type of speech. Obscenities are restricted in public media and most formal communication systems. However offensive, the use of obscene language in public is on the rise. Here I distinguish the use of obscenities from other cursing

Repeated use of obscenities should be dealt with swiftly and stringently.

involving anger, issues of sexual harassment, and discrimination. I limit discussion to the use of obscene language ("fuck," "motherfucker," "twat," "cunt," "tits," and so forth) to ordinary communication. Language-related problems with harassment and anger are dealt with in chapters 41 and 23.

A student's first use of obscenity should result in a warning. Tell the student that obscenity is unacceptable in school and a repeat of it will result in punishment or loss of privileges. Repeated use of obscenities should be dealt with swiftly and stringently. Give the student a marker or make a notation on a note card while face-to-face with the student, indicating that the punishment will be served later. In most cases, students are given an in-school or after-school suspension. If suspensions are to be given, one or two warnings are used first. An alternative is loss of privileges such as denying attendance at an after school function like a dance, football game, or school trip. Consider the response-cost protocol for cursing presented in Part Five.

- Obscenity is unacceptable. The first incidence receives a warning, and subsequent usage results in suspensions or loss of privileges

- Severe behavior problems are appearing in "normal" classrooms, and teachers and staff must have a plan to deal with confrontational and defiant students who use offensive language

Cases

Here are a few cases involving obscenity. What would you do if this happened to you? What would you say? Take time to write down your reaction or solution to each case before looking at the suggested responses.

Jerry

Tom and Jerry are walking into the classroom before class. You are sitting at your desk, and both boys look at you. Then Jerry says to Tom, "I didn't finish the fuckin' homework."

Cathy

You are walking by the women's restroom, and you hear a familiar voice say, "I hate that guy. He's a fuckin' pussy." You enter the restroom and see one of your students, Cathy, talking to her friends.

Tom

As school ends on a rainy day, the students are getting their coats and hurrying off to the school buses. Running out the door, Tom drops his notebook in a puddle and says to himself, "What a fucking mess." You are walking down the hallway inside the building but can hear what he said. He does not see you, and no other students are around him.

The Whole Group

You enter your classroom on Monday morning to find about half of your students listening to and singing the lyrics of a sexually explicit rap song called "Bad Ass Bitch." The group seems embarrassed when you come in the room, but they keep singing and playing the music.

Darnell

Darnell is a foster child who has moved to your small community from a big city school. He is one year older and much taller than your other students. After you give an assignment, Darnell says, "Teach, this is a bunch of bullshit. I ain't gonna do all this bullshit homework." You tell Darnell that his language is inappropriate and that you will talk to him after class. He says, "It's still bullshit, and I ain't doin' a fuckin' thing." The other boys in the class are smirking and it seems clear that the problem is escalating. You ask him to go to the principal's office, but he refuses and keeps cursing you in front of the class.

Raymond

Raymond is one of your students with an attention deficit disorder. In the past, he would be referred to as a hyperactive student and placed in a special education class. With your state's inclusion policy, Raymond is now in your class. Usually he behaves, but today he is shouting, "Fuck, fuck, cunt, fuck," and struggling to get away from the classroom aide. The other students are becoming increasingly distracted by the episode and are watching to see what you will do.

Responses

Here are possible responses to the foregoing cases.

Jerry

Jerry has used an obscenity right in front of you, and you must respond to the language. If he has not been warned before, give him a warning this time. If he has received fair warning, then you should punish him, give him a marker, make a notation on a note card (for a later suspension), or indicate that he has lost privileges. These consequences should be covered in the school's written policy on obscenity.

Cathy

You did not observe who said the obscenity, and it would be proper to ignore the episode. There is no need to assert authority over the whole group, as in trying to punish all of them for the carelessness of one student. Let it ride this time.

Tom

Tom is upset and has expressed his anger in a common way. It may be best to ignore the episode or ask Tom if he needs some help with his notebook. He may not even be aware of what he said due to his emotional state.

The Whole Group

You have to respond to the entire group of students involved in the incident. If the school has a written policy on obscenity, offer a warning. Remind all that a repeat of the behavior results in a group loss of privileges or after-school suspension during which they can help you clean up the classroom. Consult the school's policy about playing explicit music on campus.

Darnell

This is not only a cursing problem but an episode of defiant or oppositional conduct. Deal with Darnell's behavior first. If you think he will go voluntarily to the principal's office, send him immediately. You can ask another student to go with him to make sure Darnell goes to the office. If he will not go voluntarily, send another student or your aide to tell the principal to come immediately to remove Darnell from your room since he cannot and will not go to the principal's office alone. After you or the principal deal with the oppositional conduct, then the issue of unacceptable language can be addressed.

Some behavior problems escalate when you give them attention. Keep in mind that teachers must be careful not to grab or physically restrain students. Some state laws prohibit such physical contact. It is probably best to get the principal and perhaps another person who has been trained to deal with physically abusive students to remove cursing and defiant students from your classroom. You never know what is bothering some students or what has angered them earlier in the day.

Raymond

Have the aide take Raymond to a timeout area or a secluded part of the room and try to calm him down. If there is no timeout area or space, take him into the hall until he calms down. If Raymond continues to curse and disrupt the class, take him to the school's counselor.

Some schools have set aside a "resource room" for inclusion students who want to work there. The student's parents would have to sign a statement that they agreed that the student could do his or her work (but not play) in the resource room when he or she volunteers to do so. Some inclusion students, for example, prefer to work in the resource room rather than attend physical education classes.

Summary

Extreme language in the form of obscenity or defiant behavior is unacceptable, and its use generally results in punishment. Have a plan to deal with extreme language and be prepared to use other staff members' help when necessary.

CHAPTER 41

Dealing with Sexual Harassment and Gender Issues

Sexual harassment is a form of discrimination, and hence, federal courts have forbidden such behavior in the general workplace, including public schools. Schools are being held responsible for monetary damages awarded to students who have been harassed at school.

The most obvious forms of sexual harassment, such as asking for sexual favors for grades or touching other people, are easy to identify. Sexual harassment based on language is less clear. The school should distribute a copy of the EEOC statement regarding sexual harassment (I quoted this policy in Part One) and give concrete examples of what constitutes unwanted sexual remarks and jokes of a sexual nature. These documents should be given to teachers and students to be reviewed in class, allowing time for class discussion. Students should be given a handbook at the beginning of the year stating what behaviors are sanctioned at school and what corrective measures are used. Point systems for punishment and in-school and after-school suspensions are described.

While parents may interpret comments about sexual behavior or appearance or sexual horseplay (snapping bra straps or pulling down gym shorts) as "boys will be boys," parents and students must be informed otherwise. Regardless of how parents minimize these problems, state and federal courts consider these types of behavior

Give concrete examples of what constitutes unwanted sexual remarks and jokes of a sexual nature.

to be harassment. Teachers and administrators who allow it to occur and escalate can be held accountable.

Harassment, in most cases, is based on a pattern of repeated behaviors as opposed to a single incident. The EEOC definition presents the notion that the harassing behavior is "unwanted." To be unwanted, the harassing behavior has to occur first and be experienced as unwanted by the victim. At some point after the unwanted behavior occurs, the victim has to communicate directly to the harasser or indirectly through the administration or staff that such behavior is indeed unwanted. Once the victim has complained and the harasser has been informed, a second occurrence of the harassing behavior would be considered harassment (since the harasser previously was warned that his conduct was unwanted).

Sexual harassment can occur between any two members of the school population. Teachers and administrators could harass students, or students could harass each other. All forms are illegal. The typical forms of harassment occur when a person with more power or status intimidates or takes advantage of a person with less power or status.

Resources

A formal policy with regard to harassment should identify resource people on campus (teachers, administrators, or staff) who can listen to student complaints and advise students of their alternatives (confront the harasser in person or in writing or let a third party communicate to the harasser). A list of these resource people can be included in the handbook and displayed on posters in several prime locations in the hallways. Make it clear to students what constitutes harassment and make it clear that sexual harassment is illegal.

Verbal Sexual Harassment

Verbal sexual harassment occurs when students produce comments, jokes, or insults of a sexual nature in speech or written comments. These comments may describe the appearance of a person ("Betty has big tits" or "What a nice ass"), his or her sexual behavior ("Dave is queer and sucks big dicks" or "Karen is a slut and does it on the first date"), or terms that belittle or denigrate students based on their gender or sexual preference ("honey," "whore," "slut," "cunt," "bitch," or "sweetie"). These comments could be made to victims or targets, or the comments could be hearsay and rumors about victims to other listeners. Harassing comments include graffiti and written notes passed about in school.

Unwanted joking could refer to a joke about a student who is identified within the joke. Unwanted jokes also refer to the telling of a sexual joke to someone who has asked not to hear them. The harasser victimizes the listener by telling the unwanted joke to or in front of him or her. In other words, the listeners are indeed a "captive audience."

Issues of Gender Discrimination and Sexual Orientation

Psychologists have long known that many of the gender differences that appear in our culture are not due to biological differences but are fostered by differences in social interaction and training. We need to eliminate intolerant attitudes among staff and students that result in discrimination and prevent victims from obtaining the education they deserve. Several types of problems need attention.

Denigration of Women

Older men have a tendency to denigrate women by calling them names that diminish their existence. These include "sweetie," "honey," "sugar," "pumpkin," "the little missus," and "ladies." Many regard the reference to women as "girls" to be both diminutive and denigrating. Women should inform a speaker who uses diminutive and denigrating language that such language is offensive to women and that the speaker should find a more appropriate gender-neutral reference.

Those teachers who coach boys' athletic teams must be careful not to refer to boys as "girls" or "ladies" when they are angry at the players. Putdowns of male athletes derived from references to femininity should be eliminated. Many studies show that men are less sensitive than women about the use of sexist language. While diminutive references ("honey") are milder than sexual harassment behavior, gender-related insults can be evidence of hostile working conditions, thus preventing women from working effectively.

Rap or Hip Hop Jargon

A related issue concerns urban street jargon that routinely uses the words "bitch" and "ho" to refer to women. Both boys and girls use these negative terms for women because the terms are popular in rap and dance music genres. Obviously, these should be eliminated from classroom discussions and comments. Besides eliminating these words, teachers should engage the class in a discussion which indicates why these terms are inappropriate.

Intolerance of Sexual Preferences

The main issue here is the derogation of lesbian and gay students. Students who claim they are gay or express their preferences for a gay lifestyle have been targeted and harassed in many schools. The gay student population has one of the highest rates of suicide among all teens. Some states have passed legislation to protect the rights of gay students in public schools, but most schools are far behind concerning effective intervention for gay students. Students need to be tolerant of others' sexual preferences.

- Verbal sexual harassment and gender-related insults are unacceptable, illegal, and punishable behavior.

- They promote intolerance for individual differences and respect for young women.

- Make sure the student handbook has a clear policy on harassment and discrimination.

Cases

Here are a set of cases involving the use of harassing speech. Consider the circumstances of each case. What would you do in each case? Write out a brief response to each case.

Dave

Dave comes up to you before class and is very upset. He is on the verge of tears. He asks to talk to you about something that happened in his physical education class. Two of the bigger boys started making fun of him because he had not developed any pubic hair. The boys started calling him "fag," "queer," and "bitch" and got the others in the locker room to chant along with them. Right before the team was to head out to play soccer, they pulled his pants down in front of the entire class. The physical education instructor was nearby but acted as if he heard nothing. The instructor did nothing to help Dave and would not talk to him after class. Dave came to you for help.

Betty

Betty is the first girl in your class to wear a bra and has developed breasts before any of her classmates. The boys start leering at her, rolling their eyes, and talking amongst themselves about her sex life. You let this seemingly innocent behavior go, but now when Betty comes in the room, several of the boys make mooing sounds and say words like "jugs," "udders," and "Bossie the cow." Betty is becoming very self-conscious and blushes when the boys make these comments. Today one of the boys snapped her bra in the lunch line.

Karen

Karen is a minority student from a poverty-stricken section of town. She and her friends started wearing lots of makeup, similar to the older girls from their neighborhood, before the other girls in the class. One set of girls and boys started making comments about these girls and speculating that the girls are promiscuous. Some boys have spread rumors that Karen had sex with a high school boy during the school dance. One day you are walking down the hall, and you hear a group of students saying, "Slut," "Whore," and "I bet that bitch does it" as Karen walks to her next class. Karen never complains and puts on a tough exterior when these comments occur.

Coach Ned

On your way to your car you can hear the football coach yelling at several members of the team. You hear him say, "You hit each other like a bunch of old women," and he continues his complaining with other phrases and words such as "little girls," "pussies," "pink panties football," and "bunch of fags." The next day you run into Coach Ned in the teachers' lounge where he is talking about the football team.

Eddie

Eddie has been the class clown for several years. Now he has taken to telling sexist jokes to his friends or anyone who will listen. One day before class he is telling an obscene joke about a woman forced to have sex with a policeman. The girls in the class and some of the boys look somewhat stunned that he is saying these things to a captive audience. Several students are blushing and hiding their heads.

Kate

One day "Kate is a slut" is written on the boys' bathroom wall. A few days later, other phrases are added: "Kate sucks dicks" and "Kate is a whore." Several boys begin talking about the graffiti, and eventually Kate hears about it from some of her girlfriends. At first she is reluctant to discuss the graffiti with anyone, but eventually she tells her mother. Her father becomes enraged and notifies you, her closest teacher, that unless the graffiti is removed immediately, he is going to sue the school for allowing the sexual harassment to occur.

Responses

Dave

Unless Dave will tell you who the perpetrators are, confront the entire physical education class. This type of behavior and name calling could form the basis of a sexual harassment suit if it is allowed to continue. The boys need to know that it is unacceptable to harass and insult another student in the manner that they did with Dave. The class must be warned. Another episode would result in suspension and the loss of privileges, and parents will be notified.

You must also be careful not to make the situation worse for Dave so that the boys do not retaliate against him during class or after school. The boys should be told that they are the ones who have the problem, not Dave. The physical education instructor needs to be made aware of his mistake and might need to discuss the problem with the class. If the physical education instructor is not aware of the problem, you need to make him aware. He could have stopped the incident, and it was wrong for him to ignore it.

Betty

If you feel that the class on the whole needs to be reminded about the sexual harassment policy, address the issue as a general concern without belaboring the point. If you feel that the problem will escalate, you can discuss the matter with the boys in the class and, on a separate occasion, with the girls. In each case, remind the group that students must be respectful of other people's bodies and that unwanted touching and remarks are unacceptable. Tell them that future occurrences would result in suspension and the loss of privileges.

If the problem is more specific and is the misbehavior of only a few boys, address the harassers directly, swiftly, and sternly. Here you want to be very specific about who, what, where, and when, making it clear that touching and sexist comments will not be tolerated. It should be stated that further episodes will be punished, and the parents of the harassers will be notified.

Karen

Regardless of whether or not Karen complains about these comments, the insults, comments, and speculation about her sexual promiscuity are unacceptable. If you can identify specific students who have made these comments and spread rumors about Karen, deal with the trouble makers directly and warn them. These kinds of rumors and innuendoes about others are the basis of libel and slander suits in the "real world" workplace, and such comments cannot be tolerated in school or in the real world.

This kind of episode is very common with adolescents across the country and is very difficult to eradicate. However, teachers who hear these insults and rumors must deal directly with the speakers, regardless of whether the victims ask for help.

Coach Ned

You need to pull Coach Ned aside and tell him what you heard the other day. Make it clear that you understand that he has a need to control and motivate his players, but this cannot be accomplished at the expense of womankind through derogatory comments based on femininity. Nor does he need to stigmatize and derogate gays in order to coach young boys.

Coaches are sometimes sexist, and their tactics on and off the field are difficult to change. Ned needs to be reminded that he is a role model and authority figure who greatly influences these boys, more so than some of their parents. This is a responsibility that he cannot take lightly. He must also adhere to the school's policy on sexual harassment both on and off the field.

Eddie

Deal with Eddie directly outside of the classroom situation. Warn him that future obscene and sexist comments and jokes on campus will result in suspension and the loss of privileges. While he can tell these jokes with his close friends who want to hear them, he cannot victimize the entire class, nor can he make comments that derogate women as a group.

Is this the second time Eddie (or any harasser) has gotten into trouble? If the answer is yes, give him an in-school suspension or a marker for an after-school suspension.

Kate

First, tell the principal. The principal should get a custodian and immediately remove all graffiti. If the instigator can be identified, he should be made to remove the graffiti and apologize to Kate. Notify the parents that the graffiti have been removed and that the instigator has been punished and asked to apologize to their daughter.

Summary

If a student has used an obscenity or has committed what you consider to be an act of sexual harassment, you should consider using an in-school or after-school suspension because these are serious issues and students must be sanctioned. Your job and the reputation of the school is on the line. If you can identify the student-instigator, make him apologize to the victim either in private or public, whichever is fitting. Harassment should be clearly defined in a student handbook and the policy should be discussed with students from time to time.

CHAPTER 42

Dealing with Ethnic and Racial Slurs

One of the more problematic forms of cursing is the use of words that put people down or insult students based on race, religion, or ethnic background. Psychologists and those in the legal profession have not determined exactly what impact these words have on others or if such language constitutes illegal behavior or not. Most schools prohibit the use of discriminatory speech.

Sometimes an extreme word like "nigger" is used among members of the same race without any harm intended. Whether this use is benign and should be ignored is debatable. On the other hand, there are cases where the slur could be used in a hate crime. This may indicate that the crime was premeditated on the grounds of prejudice. The use of ethnic slurs could be considered a form of discrimination as well. Obviously, contextual variables must be weighed to interpret and comprehend ethnic terms among speakers and listeners.

It would be nice if we could eliminate these references from public use. However, as long as some Americans have more power and status than others, the lower status references to appearance, religion, food preferences, music preferences, skin color, and social customs will sources of ridicule and insult. Recent immigrants have been scapegoated and insulted in the same fashion as previous immigrants throughout our history. When will it stop? We can train

Teachers need to comprehend the meaning of terms groups use against each other.

our students at the earliest possible age to respect differences. As you try to deal with ethnic differences and insults, you may want to take some class time to discuss words that hurt and why.

We can establish rules and policies that prohibit the use of extreme forms (not all forms) of ethnic slurs on campus. Mild forms of insulting are difficult to monitor and control, and making rules about mild insults would be doomed to failure. At a minimum, however, words that cause friction or incite and escalate aggression between different racial and ethnic groups on campus must be monitored. For example, students who engage in physical aggression and use ethnic slurs could receive enhanced punishment due to the use of slurs. Ethnic slurs should be eliminated from the speech of all official representatives of the school, including, athletes, coaches, cheerleaders, band members, and those representing school clubs.

Teacher awareness is an important component of monitoring and sanctioning discrimination. Teachers need to comprehend the meaning of terms groups use against each other when the members of a group are angry. If you do not know what your students are saying when they are angry, how can you tell if students are insulting each other? Do not pretend to know the meaning of words that you do recognize. Ask a student in private to define the word you do not understand.

- Ethnic and racial slurs represent prejudicial language which refers to real or apparent differences among races (skin color, religious customs, clothing, or speech).

- Racist language is unacceptable and punishable and may be illegal.

- Promote tolerance, self-esteem, and non-discrimination.

Cases

Each of these cases involves the use of ethnic and racial language. What would you do in each case?

Eric and Jeff

Right before you are ready to give a test, you hear Jeff yell to Eric, who is out in the hallway, "Hey, you fat ass nigger, get in here and take this test." Both boys are African-American and are good friends.

Wanda

In your class you are talking about bartering, trading, buying, and selling. Wanda, during the discussion about bartering, says, "You always try to jew them down to the lowest price." She continues without any realization of what she has said. A couple of Jewish students are wincing and shaking their heads.

Spike and Lee

You teach in a middle-class, Caucasian neighborhood school. Spike comes into the class with a new jacket and sneakers. Lee says, "Look here everybody. Here he comes. You look like some kinda overpaid, nigger basketball player."

Responses

Eric and Jeff

This is a tough one because there is apparently no ill will between the two boys, and they are not angry or upset. If you have a policy forbidding the use of racial language, remind the class not to use such language on campus. There is much a teacher can do to eradicate such racist language in the community, but you do have the right to forbid the use of words like "nigger" and "fat ass" in your class, regardless of the intent of the students who use these slurs.

Wanda

You do not have to pick on Wanda to solve this one. Ask the class to consider the phrase "jew down" and where the term came from. Tell the class that there are many phrases like these in English ("Indian giver," "Dutch treat," and so forth), but they reflect insensitivity and are inappropriate in the conversations of educated people. When you hear phrases such as "Indian giver" in class, take the opportunity to teach students about the origin of such language and why the use of such language is inappropriate and disrespectful.

Spike and Lee

Respond to Lee directly in front of the class, especially if students are listening or paying attention to him. Say something like, "We do not use racial insults in this class. In the future please express your opinions without using these terms." You have to take the occasion to instruct the entire class, especially since your students are mostly Caucasian, who may have little contact with other ethnic groups. You should be aware of the stereotypes and bigoted attitudes in your school. If you let this incident go without comment, you are contributing to the bigotry.

Summary

Ethnic and racial slurs are disrespectful and they generally underlie a prejudiced mind. In many cases, such language may constitute a form of discrimination that is illegal at school. As such, discriminatory language is unacceptable and must be eliminated.

CHAPTER 43

Dealing with Profanity and Blasphemy

What are the religious or language values in your community? In your school? How important is religion in the life of your students? Is your school a public school, or is it a church-affiliated private school? Unless you have a great deal of control over conduct and expression within a private church-affiliated school, controlling profanity and blasphemy is difficult.

In most communities around the country, profanity has become so common that people are hardly aware that words like "damn" or "hell" are being used inappropriately. Profanities appear in comic strips and electronic media. While extremely offensive language such as obscenity and harassment cannot be ignored due to legal implications, some mild profanities could be ignored outside of the classroom. Inside the classroom, teachers have the right to curb the use of profanity, especially if the school and community support traditional religious values.

The problem with sanctioning mildly offensive language such as slang, vulgarity, and profanity is the "policing" issue. Teachers are put in an awkward position of "language police" throughout most of the school day to stop these mildly offensive words. Would the authoritarian control of language on campus be worth the constraint of students' behavior? Would highly restrictive language codes outside of the classroom be enforceable? How would restrictive

Teachers have the right to curb the use of profanity, especially if the school and community support traditional religious values.

language codes fit with other restrictions of student behavior? Does the end result of eliminating all profanity justify the means of monitoring and controlling such behavior? Each school must decide the answers to these questions. Teachers must judge if it is necessary to monitor all speech.

The best place to control profanity is in one's classroom. In large school systems, it may be necessary to ignore anonymous usage in the hallways and during recess times as the shear frequency of these mild words makes control impossible to police. In small schools where speakers can be identified in the hallways, it is possible to deal directly with individuals, and every member of the school staff should enforce the school's rules at all times and in all places. In the end, common sense should prevail. Sometime teachers may be too stressed to deal directly with additional problems in the hallways.

In the classroom setting when someone uses "hell" or "damn," instruct students, as a class, to express their intense emotions with acceptable language as the use of profanities in restricted social settings stigmatizes the speaker as uneducated and socially inept.

Cases

What would you do in these episodes of profanity in the classroom? How would you handle each case? Write down your answers before looking at the suggested responses.

Adam

Your students are talking about the Civil War. When asked what happened at the end of the battle, Adam says, "The rest of the soldiers ran like hell."

Eve

You are conducting a normal class when outside there is a loud crash. Your students look out the window to witness a two-car collision. Eve blurts out, "Holy shit."

Responses

Adam

You have several choices here. If you think that Adam is just excited and would not repeat this word, ignore the profanity. If the class reacts with surprise to Adams's use of a profanity and they are looking at you to respond, then you have to make a statement. You want to instruct Adam that he needs to find an alternative expression to replace the profanity, for example, "Say that again without the profanity." You could repeat the rule, "We do not use profanities in the classroom setting." If any student repeats the profanity, deal with him or her more sternly.

Eve

If this is a one-time occurrence (accidents are rare by definition) and the students did not hear what Eve said, then ignore the profanity. If the class is surprised at Eve's cursing, then you have to respond. You could say, "I know you are excited, Eve, but you may not use profanities to express surprise in the classroom. Say, 'Oh, my goodness' or 'holy smoke.'" If anyone in the class repeats the profanity, dealt with him or her more sternly.

Summary

- Profanity and blasphemy are inappropriate for classroom use and unacceptable in some schools.

- Mild forms are frequently used and hard to monitor outside of the classroom.

- Confront obvious, voluntary uses and ignore non-obtrusive expressions of surprise.

Dealing with Slang

To deal with slang, you have to know what it is. To know what slang is, you have to be informed about the groups who use it. You can catch up with current jargon by consuming your students' popular culture. You can scan one of several good reference books on slang. In the end, one can never know all the slang and jargon that is in use, but you can try to keep informed about the words used in your school. You can ask your colleagues and students what slang words mean and spend class time discussing modern slang. Students need to know why both standard language and slang are used to communicate in the modern world.

One important note: do not pretend to know words that you are unfamiliar with and do not try to speak in a different dialect if you do not know how to do so. If you use dialects and slang inappropriately, students will see that you are a phony. Using slang may bring you closer to students, but it sends a message that slang is appropriate in school because the teacher used it.

Teachers should hold students to conventional language standards for written assignments but not punish students who speak different dialects. Sometimes teachers confuse dialect differences with the use of slang, but dialect and slang are not the same form of speech. Dialects have different rules for pronunciation or word endings and are difficult to change. Slang is basically unconventional vocabulary and is easier to change. Remember that slang develops within groups to solidify in-group communication and trust while at the same time distancing the group from non-group members.

Students should be taught that slang is inappropriate for certain communications between educated people.

Slang is not necessarily bad; it is a natural reaction of people socializing in groups. As such, teachers cannot eliminate slang and probably should not be too concerned about slang terms except terms that are indecent or unacceptable for written communication. Students should be taught that slang is inappropriate for certain communications among educated people. Those who aspire to work in media and entertainment, retailing, sales, and most business settings cannot use slang on a regular basis. Those who travel abroad or communicate with foreigners find slang to have an extremely limited usage. Students need to find alternatives for slang. Students who use or overuse slang must be challenged to produce the same thought in conventional language: "How would you say that without using the word 'X?'"

A slang problem may occur for individual students or for a major portion of your class. For some students, switching from slang to conventional expressions may be simple, but for others, who may be bombarded with slang throughout the day, switching may not be as easy. For heavy slang users, instruction in more conventional expressions is necessary. Teach students to substitute an appropriate phrase for one which too slangy.

Cases

Here are a few cases of slang usage to practice your problem-solving skills. Try to resolve the issues in writing before looking at the suggested responses.

Jan and Dean

Two of your students are playing on skateboards at lunch. "Bitchin' ride, dude," Dean says to Jan as they whip by you near the swings.

Jimmy and Cliff

In the spring, many of your students like to wear colorful T-shirts. You arrive at your first class, where Cliff is sitting in the front row with a T-shirt that reads, "Coed Naked Football." Jimmy has a T-shirt with a marijuana leaf on the front and a picture of his favorite band on the back.

Taysha

After class one day, Taysha comes up to your desk with a worried look on her face. "He be dissin' me and runnin' me down in front of my set," she says. You have no idea what she is talking about, and you ask her to say it again. She repeats, "He be dissin' me, Mrs. Smith, real bad." She runs off crying.

Misty

You are observing your homeroom class as they leave the room. You notice that Misty has written "Joe is a dickhead" on her book cover. You also see that she has written the same phrase on the back of her hand in ink. Her girlfriends have noticed the writing and make comments about how Joe treats every girl with disrespect.

Dona

Dona has always worn provocative clothing and jewelry. She tries to get other students' attention, and she comments about the things she wears to school. Today she arrives with a necklace that spells out "bitch." She also has a tattoo on her arm, representing a naked man and naked woman embracing. You notice the necklace and tattoo once you enter your classroom.

Responses

Jan and Dean

Unless it was obvious to you that the boys were trying to get your attention by using the word "bitchin'," you can ignore this episode. "Bitchin'" is a term that is used frequently in music and video cultures and has been increasingly used in media and advertisements. However, if you think the use was intentional and that they wanted to get your attention or provoke you, tell the boys to find another word to express their exuberance. Many slang episodes will require your judgment.

Jimmy and Cliff

Many schools have a policy about vulgar T-shirts. These policies usually request that the student do one of the following: (a) turn the T-shirt inside out, (b) find another shirt, or (c) go home to get another shirt. Every school has a different threshold for T-shirt humor. You should know your school's threshold.

Taysha

You cannot act like you know what is going on because you do not understand the situation. Taysha may already sense your confusion. The problem is that you do not know street jargon well enough to understand that Taysha has been and is being picked on and put down in front of her girlfriends. How can you translate? Ask another student or a colleague what the expressions mean. Consult a slang dictionary or consult a counselor. You could ask Taysha specifically what "dissin'" means. When you determine what the problem is, take Taysha aside. Confess your initial confusion about her problem. Ask her what she would like you to do to help her with her problem now that you understand what her complaint is.

Misty

Catch up to Misty and take her aside from her friends. Tell her you need to speak to her in private. Remind her about the school policy about inappropriate language and tell her to remove the book cover or cover the phrase with tape. Tell her to wash her hands immediately and remove the ink.

Dona

Approach Dona and ask to speak to her alone immediately before class begins. If you let this problem go, she will continue to get attention from her classmates and will disrupt the class. The necklace problem is easy. Tell her to remove it for the rest of the day and tell her never to wear the necklace at school again. Is the tattoo real or temporary? If it is temporary (such tattoos are popular these days), tell her to remove it immediately. If it is permanent, tell her that she must keep the tattoo covered during school hours.

Summary

- Slang is very common, but offensive slang is inappropriate for classrooms.

- Be knowledgeable about the meanings of slang words you hear.

- Promote the use of conventional language for assignments.

- Mild forms are acceptable as language changes over time.

CHAPTER 45

Dealing with Vulgar Language

Vulgar language is inappropriate for educated people interacting in formal settings. Vulgarities are not bad or illegal; they are used very frequently in everyday language by people on the street. There is nothing wrong with knowing and using vulgarities per se; however, students must know the appropriate conventional terms and words to communicate effectively in constrained situations. Speaking in public, communicating to customers, talking to your employer, conducting a job interview, and consulting with a physician or counselor all require conventional English. When a speaker uses vulgarities, he or she is perceived as vulgar person.

Students need to know that using vulgar language prevents them from climbing the social ladder and getting the kinds of jobs they want. One good argument against the use of vulgarity is that it could cost a person his or her job. Bosses who have the power to hire could fire a student for the use of improper language at work. A student needs to know that he or she has some responsibility to use conventional language in the classroom and certainly in any written materials for the teacher. These are not merely the teachers' standards, but they are the standards of your school system and of education in general. Vulgar language is like casual clothing. You cannot use either in formal settings.

The best approach to dealing with vulgar language is the instructional approach. When a student uses a vulgar term, inform all the students, not just the speaker, that vulgarities are inappropriate and that more acceptable substitutes must be explored.

You have to instruct students about what terms are acceptable replacements for vulgarities.

As with slang, the ability to switch from a vulgar style of speaking to a conventional style may be easy for some students but difficult for others. If a student comes from a family, peer, or community environment that is filled with vulgar manners of speech, you have to instruct students about what terms are acceptable replacements for vulgarities. Some students may resist changing their vulgar ways as it may be viewed as an attack on their social status or social group. Do not think that you can completely eliminate vulgar speech; it is just too common.

Cases

Examine each of these cases and write out how you would react to each before you read the suggested responses.

Loretta

During the first week of classes, Loretta comes up to your desk before class starts and asks to be moved to another part of the room. When you question her further about why this move is necessary, Loretta says, "Because that guy in front of me smells like dog crap."

Willy

During your class, Willy raises his hand. Instead of asking to go to the restroom, as others usually ask, he says, "Teacher, I have to pee real bad." The rest of the class starts laughing loudly, and some begin repeating out loud, "I have to pee real bad."

Paul

During a discussion about food preferences, Paul remarks that he does not like pudding because it reminds him of "snot." When you ask him to describe pudding again without using "that word," he gets a confused look on his face and then turns red and looks down at his desk without answering.

Bob and Ray

During a class, you notice that Bob and Ray are passing a note back and forth between each other and quietly laughing. You walk down the aisle and quietly take the note from Bob. At the end of the class, you read the note and find that they have been exchanging insults in writing: "dickhead," "dillweed," "fuzzbutt," "dorkwad," "asswipe," and so forth. The students have all left the room by the time you figure out what was going on.

Responses

Loretta

Tell Loretta that she can be moved but that she should refer to the student in front of her as having a foul odor or a bad smell. Remind her that the word "crap" is vulgar and that some more polite term must be substituted.

Willy

Tell Willy that the next time he has "to urinate" he should ask for a restroom pass. Tell him the class does not need to know the details of his business in the restroom.

Paul

It would appear that Paul is on the spot. Better talk to him later, away from the classroom context. Ask him if he has trouble finding acceptable words from time to time. If he appears receptive, pursue the matter further. Tell him he could have used words like "gooey" or "slippery" and if he wants to sound educated, he could use "viscous."

Bob and Ray

This is a mild infraction, but one with which you should deal. Bob and Ray should be taken aside and told that note passing is disruptive and that future incidents will lead to suspension. The language is another issue. They should be told that this type of slang has no place in the classroom in spoken or written form and if they want to insult each other in a childish manner with such language to do so when they are not in school.

Summary

- Offensive forms of vulgar speech are inappropriate for classroom use.

- Promote conventional standards for classroom assignments.

- Mild vulgarities may be acceptable but ask for alternatives.

- Convince students that conventional speech is more desirable.

CHAPTER 46

Summing Up: Cursing and Context

Most of us learn to speak with such ease that we never take time to examine just how complex human communication is. Language is a rule-governed system of interacting components, including phonological, syntactic, pragmatic, and semantic subsystems. Aspects of language usage must be understood by considering these underlying language systems within social and physical contexts. Cursing is only one way in which humans communicate with each other in different environments. Importantly, cursing, as a form of communication, cannot be understood without carefully examining the contexts in which it occurs. There is no form of communication more sensitive to context than cursing. We must know the who, what, where, and when to understand why students curse and how cursing affects others.

I will conclude this book by briefly examining contextual variables that teachers must consider to effectively deal with students' bad language. Simply put, the next time you hear an episode of bad language usage at school ask yourself the following questions:

- *Why* did he or she say that?
- *Who* said the offensive words and to whom?
- *What* words were chosen?

We must know the who, what, where, and when to understand why students curse and how cursing affects others.

- *Where* did the episode take place?
- *When* did the episode occur?
- *How* should I deal with the incident?

Context is everything.

Why

Many teachers and parents react to children's bad language without first asking what motivated the child to use it. If a student uses an expression of anger, first assess why the student is angry. Deal with the anger and emotion first and then the bad language. With episodes of name calling, insulting, profanity, obscenity, or slang, ask yourself why students used the words they did. What is the motivation to curse?

I have presented many reasons why students use bad language. Sometimes the use of bad language is a conditioned, primitive reaction to frustration or threats. Other times, the language is controlled and strategic, as when a student writes graffiti on a wall. When you are looking for reasons why students curse, consider the chapters covering anger, role models, popular culture, slang, ethnic slurs, attention seeking, and negative identity development.

Who

Some students are more prone to cursing than others, and there are many psycho-social reasons why one student is more motivated to curse than others. Teachers generally have a pretty good understanding of individual differences and use this information to treat individual students accordingly. One student may be having a bad day, another may have a history of aggressive outbursts, and a third may have to be forced or provoked into cursing. Remember that the language is bad but not necessarily the students who use it.

What

Parts One, Two, and Three demonstrate clearly that students produce different types of cursing (slang, obscenity, profanity, sexual harassment, and ethnic slurs). Speakers also have different language values underlying their word choices (national, regional, and local values). Some types of cursing are more offensive and problematic than other ones. Sexual harassment and discrimination cannot be tolerated and are unacceptable at school. On the other hand, mild forms of slang and profanity are so widespread that many teachers have chosen not to respond to every single instance of cursing. School policy and teachers' standards determine what is acceptable in a classroom. It is best for both students and teachers to have clear definitions of unacceptable language stated in a student handbook. With clear rules and definitions, teachers and students will be aware when the rules are broken and what penalties will be given for breaking the rules.

Where

Adult speakers are generally sensitive to where they are talking. We know what speech is acceptable or what is inappropriate in a given setting. What teachers can say while driving home is different than what they can say in a classroom. Similarly, students are instructed that behavior and language standards depend on where they are speaking. A teacher can control a student's language at school but not on the street corner. Teachers have the duty to control language in the classroom. Most students respect teachers' rules. However, when teachers are not present, and students are on the move, students are more likely to use foul language. Teachers recognize the students who follow the rules in the classrooms and those who curse in the hallways, bathrooms, playground, and cafeteria. A teacher can confront any student who curses in his or her presence but would be challenged to deal with every instance of cursing outside of the classroom setting. Speech offensiveness depends heavily on context.

When

The time of day and prior hassles influence a student's use of bad language. All teachers know that any student can experience a bad day now and then. Some children just get tired and cranky at the end of the school day and are likely to lose control.

Cursing occurs during periods of stress and during periods of freedom. Students are stressed by difficult classes, but not all courses are challenging. Students are likely to be vocal during physical education classes where they experience both freedom and stress. Students are likely to curse between class times, during lunch, and traveling to and from school. Students are also affected by holidays, sporting events, impending weekends and free time, and substitute teachers. Although they are not as important as other variables which affect language, time of day and events throughout the day affect bad language usage.

How Should I React?

Taking the previous variables into consideration, the most pressing chore for teachers who hear students talking dirty is to decide how to respond to dirty words. I outlined the cognitive-behavior techniques in Part Five. Those strategies and recommendations provide a variety of alternatives. I recognize that teachers manage behavior as well as instruct students about speaking appropriately. Dealing with cursing is just one of many behaviors and types of language teachers must control. The specific problems studied in chapters 40-45 allow you to put your experience and the recommendations in this book to use. Most readers find the exercises helpful.

I urge teachers to anticipate language problems and act from day one to prevent problems with clear rules and consistent reinforcement. Consider a range of strategies and select the appropriate strategy according to the type of dirty language students use.

This book was written to give you more control over students' language behavior in your classrooms. When you perceive yourself as an effective instructor and manager of behavior, you gain a sense of self-efficacy and experience less personal stress. I hope all readers gain the rewards of increased self-efficacy and less stress through a better understanding of why students curse and a knowledge of what to do when students talk dirty.

Training for a Better Community

LOOKING IN, REACHING OUT:
A Manual for Training Service Volunteers

Dorine and Ret Thomas

Looseleaf with binder, 192 pages, 8½" x 11", ISBN 0-89390-376-0

Service learning is a wonderful process, but students need to be trained to ensure that they—and those they are assigned to help—have good experiences. This manual is a complete, ready-to-go course for training service volunteers in school or community settings. Part One focuses on developing self-awareness and preparing emotionally for service work. Part Two focuses on developing specific skills such as listening, asking questions, responding, problem-solving, decision-making, and giving feedback. Part Three focuses on building group-identity and collaboration skills. All activities have been thoroughly tested over several years. Looseleaf format has everything you need to train service volunteers, including handout masters with permission to photocopy.

THE PEER HELPING TRAINING COURSE

Joan Sturkie & Maggie Phillips

Looseleaf with binder, 263 pages, 8½" x 11", ISBN 0-89390-311-6

Teenagers often find it easier to talk about their problems and issues with other students. By helping teens identify and talk about their issues, peer helpers also learn something about themselves. *The Peer Helping Training Course* helps teens learn how to be there for each other. This practical training course is divided into two sections. Part One (Units 1-9) introduces the skills students need to be good communicators. Part Two (Units 10-23) deals with specific problems such as peer pressure, drugs, death, and AIDS. Appendices contain a sample letter to parents of peer helpers, glossary, community resources, and an excellent bibliography.

Call 1-800-736-7600 for current prices.
See last page for ordering information.

Discussion-Starting Skits & Activities

FACING VIOLENCE:
Discussion-Starting Skits for Teenagers

R. William Pike

Paper, 192 pages, 6" x 9", ISBN 0-89390-344-2

Teens have many reasons for acting up. Trouble at home. Trouble with relationships. Trouble on the streets. You can get them to talk about their problems and explore solutions by using simple dramas. *Facing Violence*, part of the ACTING IT OUT series, provides you with 40 skits addressing violence in schools, violence in the home, violent language, violence and dating, violence and bias, violence in society, and solutions. Try them. They work!

FACING SUBSTANCE ABUSE:
Discussion-Starting Skits for Teenagers

R. William Pike

Paper, 192 pages, 6" x 9", ISBN 0-89390-374-4

Tobacco. Alcohol. Drugs. These substances threaten the lives of teenagers today. The danger comes not only from how they use controlled substances but from the prevalence of abuse among their families and friends. Teenagers need to know how to respond. With these real-to-life skits, which can be performed without props or rehearsal, you can get young people to work out practical ways to respond to the substance abuse in their lives. Contains more than 40 skits which have been developed and tested in high school settings.

Order from your local bookseller, or contact:

 Resource Publications, Inc.
160 E. Virginia Street #290-TR
San Jose, CA 95112-5876
1-800-736-7600 (voice)
1-408-287-8748 (fax)